Looking Back in Salt Cay

Preserving our life, our history, our legacy

PATRONELLA BEEN

Copyright © 2016 Patronella Been
ISBN 978-0-9971980-5-8

All Rights Reserved

All Rights Reserved. No part of this book may be reproduced or transmitted in any form or by any means, electronically or mechanically, including photocopying, recording, or by an information storage and retrieval system without permission in writing from the author of this book.

Layout & Design:
Tarsha L. Campbell

Published by:
DOMINIONHOUSE Publishing & Design, LLC
P.O. Box 681938 | Orlando, Florida 32868 | 407.703.4800
www.mydominionhouse.com

The Lord gave the Word: great was the company
of those who published it. (Psalms 68:11)

Table of Contents

Dedication 5

Preface 7

Chapter 1: Introduction 8

Chapter 2: About Salt Cay 12

Chapter 3: The Salt Industry. 24

Chapter 4: Our Homes – Our Abodes 36

Chapter 5: Precious Provisions 45

Chapter 6: Simplistic Joy and Serene Peace 59

Chapter 7: Entertainment and Amusements 66

Chapter 8: Transportation and Communication . . 81

Chapter 9: Religion and Church Activities 90

Chapter 10: School and Education 97

Chapter 11: Civic Groups and Organizations . . . 105

Chapter 12: Special Events 110

Chapter 13: Very Important People and Places . . 116

Table of Contents

Chapter 14: All This and More Made
Salt Cay Unique 128

Conclusion 129

An Anthology of Songs & Poems We Enjoyed at School
and in the Community During the Yester Years . 131

Bibliography 144

Acknowledgements 145

About the Author 146

Contact the Author 147

Dedication

I take pleasure in writing this book that I am dedicating to my three loving children: Gregston, Grethen, and Grescelle Been, and I hope that my grandchildren will also catch the excitement as they read it. I really want my children and the generation that follows to know what it was like growing up in Salt Cay during my childhood days and to know about the many experiences and challenges that helped to shape my future as I grew into adulthood.

Whenever I would talk about the old times my children would always say, "I can't understand how you all made it in those days; how did you handle that kind of living?" One of my daughters had a glimpse of the olden days when hurricane Ike passed our way in Grand Turk and she found it very difficult to adjust to the kerosene lamp, no running water, and especially the darkness, so she relocated to Providenciales until the conditions improved. Now, I was only born in 1948, so this book is but a SNIPPET of the history from the early nineteen hundreds moving forward to my adult years. I heard and learnt of the early years from others that are older for which I am grateful, and I grew up experiencing most of those same things for myself. Therefore the contents of this book will put me in the centre of those good old days that I enjoyed living in Salt Cay. I'm sharing what really comes to my mind and some things are a bit hard to explain in words so I tried putting a picture here and there. Children, I know you would never really understand it all, but it was a time of good childhood upbringing and fun, and adult years of learning and pressing on to reach my goals. I invite you along with all my readers to sit back, relax, and enjoy a time of **LOOKING BACK IN SALT CAY.**

Preface

Life in the tranquil little Island of Salt Cay in the earlier years was quite different from the way we live now, even though there are some things that just haven't changed. People who were born in the second half of the 1800's and saw the 1900's have experienced many changes and those who made it to the twenty-first century have seen many drastic changes transpire during their lifetime, so I want to thank Almighty God for granting me the privilege to experience so much as I grew up in Salt Cay with my parents, my siblings, relatives, and friends. The past years in Salt Cay can be considered the good old years in comparison to the 80's and up to this present time. There is nothing to replace one's childhood and youthful days, for they are times to enjoy, especially when you can LOOK BACK and reminisce or even read about it in a book such as this. I trust that my readers will have fun reading this book, for it's meant to make you laugh and get excited as you read some important and interesting facts. As you walk down memory lane with me, I want you to read as if we are having a conversation because I can only tell you what happened in my day.

CHAPTER 1

INTRODUCTION

The beautiful sun with its golden rays rising over the dewy green hills of Salt Cay always seemed to smile on us as we began our early morning chores. Some folks would welcome its brightness while chopping wood, carrying buckets of water, preparing a coal kiln, or starting housework. Others, perhaps with a shovel and rake walking toward the salt ponds, or a carpenter with his tool box in his hand going to work on a house, and the excited shopkeeper is getting that first cup of tea in a hurry to open the little store at 7 o'clock. No matter what the daily task, everyone was eager to face a day well on its way. These were days of Simplistic Joy and years of Serene Family Living. We never heard such words like drugs, homosexuality, crack addicts, cults, masked gunmen, or ever had to fear gunshots. Words such as these did not dominate the everyday conversations of persons in the home or community. We didn't hear any horns tooting or parents shouting, "Turn that television off and come before I leave you!" What we probably heard was "Hurry; get out of here before the ball goes up and you'll be late for school." In the evening we would hear, "Make sure the lamp and matches are on the table and bring the flashlight." In Salt Cay we developed our

Introduction

own dialect and used words that perhaps were never heard in the other islands. You will meet up with such words as you read this book, but do not try to find the meanings in any dictionary; they are **island words**.

Folks had their good and bad days in whatever life had to offer just as we do now, and the minor stealing habits were not even considered criminal offenses. There was probably an accident or two and that's about it. There were times when sicknesses swung like a pendulum from family to family, and happiness went down the gully. Sorrow, pain, and grief seemed to cling to some families as death seized their loved ones. But through it all the people knew how to pull themselves together and get on with life without seeking paid counsellors or having to deal with doctors' bills and expensive funeral arrangements. People of those days exercised much faith as they trusted in the power of Almighty God.

As we walked about, the evergreen cedars, palms, olive-bush, cordia, oleander, acacia and tamarind trees seemed to honour us as they bowed and waved; some seemed to whistle as the cool gentle breezes passed through them. The wind gliding across the sea brought waves of sentimental lush in our faces as the beautiful sunshine lit up the sky and the clouds floated along whether they were white or grey. We always enjoyed the rain as we looked forward to hearing pitter-patter on our housetop as the thunder rolled and lightning flashed. One time during my childhood days we heard something like rocks falling on the housetop; we learned afterward that it was pieces of ice. Of course we didn't know that it was hail so we said that it was raining blocks of ice. The pink briny water in the ponds was beautiful to look upon as the salt particles formed and sparkled like diamonds in the blazing sun.

Horses, donkeys, and cows along with their young paraded the streets from hill to town. Most of them were quite tame and friendly and were kept in the family yards in a closed area (pen) as domestic animals. The horses and donkeys were our means of transportation to pull carts and carry loads. Pigs, cows, hens, and roosters were reared for food. Our usual pets were cats, dogs, fowls, and chickens moving about in the yards and nearby surroundings, along with a few turkeys and guinea-chicks here and there.

Introduction

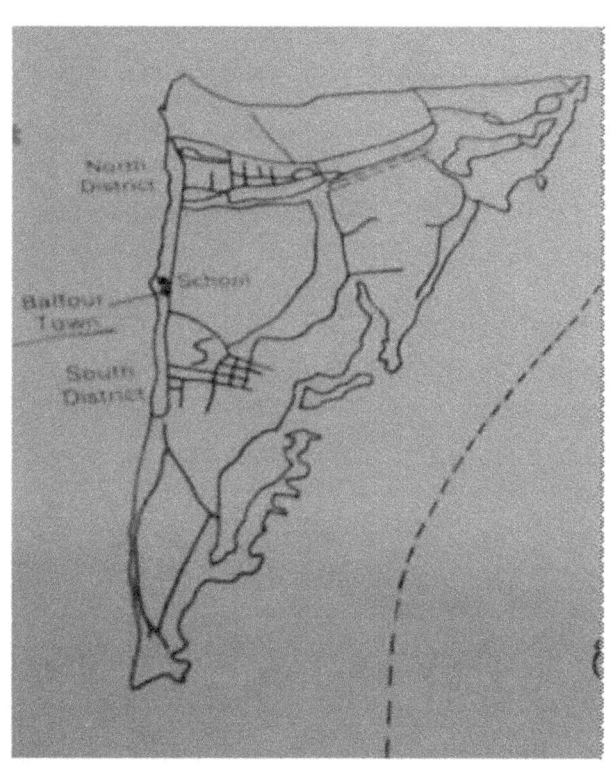

Fig. 1 - Map of Salt Cay

CHAPTER 2

ABOUT SALT CAY

Before you begin reading about some of the experiences and happenings of my little Sunkist Island home, I would like to share a synopsis of the history of Salt Cay, which is a part of the Turks and Caicos Islands. Salt Cay is just one of the inhabited islands in the Turks & Caicos chain situated 9 miles due south of Grand Turk, the capital. It is believed that Salt Cay was discovered five years before Grand Turk. It has a triangular shape, or more like the handle of an admiral's sword, with an area of 2.5 square miles. Salt Cay is comparatively flat with the rocky east coast rising up to 25 feet above sea level and sloping gradually to the west. This Island was known to be one of the world's finest SALT (White Crystal) producing locations and one can still see the remains of its 114 acres of salt ponds in the centre of the island that is referred to as the Salinas. It is one of the salt islands and therefore derived its name because it was a little CAY producing lots of SALT.

The little map of Salt Cay is just to give those who have never visited, an idea of its shape and show some points from which I will be sharing my experiences.

When the Turks and Caicos Islands shared governmental administration with Jamaica and Bahamas under British Colonial rule, Jamaican currency was in circulation in pounds (£) shillings (s) and pence (d) along with United Kingdom silver and copper coins. Those were the times when we even used half-pennies and farthings. After Jamaica obtained independence in 1962 their currency changed and in 1969 dollars ($) and cents (¢) were their own legal tender and we began using it also. We used Jamaican currency even while we were linked to the Bahamas until their Independence in 1973; then we began spending United States dollars and cents.

During the early years Turks & Caicos Islands was a dependency of Jamaica, so we shared Governors, Commissioners, and Administrators right up to their time of Independence. We also shared Governors from Bahamas until they gained Independence. Both these countries were under British colonial rule, so when they gained Independence, these Islands then came under direct colonial British rule and Governors and Administrators began coming from the United Kingdom. All Commissioners and Administrators were selected by the Secretary of State for the colonies and appointed by the Governor of that time. Salt Cay always had officials visiting from the United Kingdom as well as from Jamaica and Bahamas.

The local Government of the day constituted the Legislative Council and the Legislative Assembly with the seat of Government in Grand Turk. From the early 1950's until the mid 70's there were honourable men that represented Salt Cay as nominated and elected members or served on the Legislative Boards. They were James Morgan, James Bassett, Thaddeus Taylor, and the last elected man serving under the old constitution in the Legislative Assembly was Hon. Alexander Smith. The head of the island was the Government Officer and in 1976 under the new constitution there were a few changes. You can read about these changes in the chapter Very Important People.

Many civic developments took place in Salt Cay when the overseas officials and their wives made visits to the island occasionally. It was in the 1960's during the visit of Her Royal Highness The Princess Royal that our Girl Guides and Boy Scouts were invited to Grand Turk to form a *guard of honour* and it was an honourable occasion for Salt Cay. Lady Huggins, the wife of Governor Huggins from Jamaica, had been very instrumental in creating the Women's Federation Centre, giving them financial and moral support.

It was one of the Medical Doctors who organized the Child Welfare Association that continued for many, many years. He also had weekly Baby Clinics going in Salt Cay and a government milk scheme to distribute subsidized milk to all young children under 6 years of age. During those times it was the doctors who coordinated fund raising activities in order to keep these groups functioning and to have the children's Christmas party every year. It was persons with great ideas who helped the people in Salt Cay to develop and move forward.

In the first half of the 1900's Salt Cay had a good population of 300 and this number increased up to 450 by 1960. This was because people came from other islands to work in the salt industry during those years and children even came to attend the Elementary School thus contributing to the increase. There were many houses and families in Salt Cay and everyone kept their surroundings and the island clean. The numbers started to decrease when children began attending the Secondary School in Grand Turk and entire families moved away.

Salt Cay is divided into two districts having the ponds in the middle, and the school was located in the Balfour Town area, so as children we made separation and segregation about a lot of things especially during school days when there used to be quarrels and fights against north and south children. When any two children began fussing, someone came with a handful of sand holding it between both parties. When one would knock the sand toward the other, we shouted "Hot sand!" and big fight started when school was dismissed. Children even tore one another's clothes. Yes, there were some naughty boys and girls around during our times. I can even recall that there were fights among teachers. Shu...Shu...!!!

OUR PRODUCE

There were many little fruits growing in Salt Cay that we enjoyed. From the cactus we would pick some small fruit that we called figs. We had lots of wild sea grapes, black caicos (caucus) plums, yellow hug nuts, English-cherries, bird cherries, tamarinds, guineps, and cock-sparrows. We looked forward to the seasons when the trees would be blooming and we could go in the bush and pick some of these little fruits that were very delicious and nutritious. We could also find lots of pears on the prickly pear bush trees and we enjoyed eating them, while our mothers used the plant for food to cook some delicious pear bush n rice or buds n rice. At certain times we would walk along the beaches picking almonds and coconuts that usually drifted on the bay, especially on the northern side, but we really had no idea where they were coming from.

IMPORTS and SALES

There were a few small grocery shops located in both districts and a couple of dry good shops were on the island as well. In these little shops one could find all kinds of fabrics: broadcloth, taffeta, organdy, silk, prints, cottons, and nylon. One could buy thread, ribbon, belts, fastenings, and hooks n eyes for clothing, along with lots of buttons and elastic. Not many zippers were around then. They sold lamps and lamp shades, lanterns, and flashlights, along with other needed provisions. There were many people in Salt Cay with sewing machines who tried to make their children's clothes; in fact that was the only way most folks got clothes as they couldn't go to any store to purchase clothes during those days.

There were other miscellaneous items like Khus-Khus perfumes and soaps like LUX, LIFEBUOY, and PALMOLIVE that we called "sweet soaps" and tins of body powder: Talcum,

Mavis, and Bouquet with sweet scent. There were belts, handkerchiefs, toothbrushes, hair grease, and ring combs of all colours that gave us a lovely ponytail hairstyle. There were lots of other hair accessories that were used at that time. Hair nets were popular; if you were a grownup you could use one to make your roll in your hair along with some snaps and hair pins. Medicines such as Indian root pills, senna, herbs tea, liniment, wicks, and magnesia could also be found in the dry-good shops. There were school provisions: the little grey leaves copy books, slates with long pencils to write with, also fountain and stick pens and pencils. Bottles of blue ink and blotting paper could be found there, and guess what? You bought sheets of paper and an envelope whenever you were going to write a letter, which wasn't very often. All these supplies were Jamaican products. Our parents bought sweet soap that we only bathed with on Sundays; during weekdays we had to use the common soap that was used for washing clothes. Oh my, those were the days, but thank God for them.

The shops also carried special items and goodies for the Christmas season such as tops, the little paddle and ball, jack-in-the-box, some marbles, little plastic harmonicas (flutinas), some little dolls and tea-sets, slates, pencils, and enamel plates and matching mugs. There would also be lots of whistles, toy horns, and balloons.

The grocery shops carried 100-pound bags of sugar and flour, 50-pound sacks of rice and peas to sell at retail. There were canisters of lard and barrels of salt pork and salt beef.

I don't recall much canned foods being sold, but surely there were condensed milk and corned beef on the shelves. The folks of the day loved butter and cheese; the butter was shipped in large tins and cheese was in the usual-sized tins, but much softer and tastier. The shops had no refrigerators during these years, but lots of cakes were often made with butter rather than margarine and the butter was always soft and ready to use; it didn't melt. Nearly everything was shipped in bulk: the tea, cocoa, baking powder, yeast, and even raisins were sold in little cone-shaped packages twisted by the shopkeepers. There weren't any junk foods to purchase so we had no choice but to eat healthy.

A BEAUTIFUL SCENE OF THE SALINAS

Fig. 2 - The Salinas

The island was beautiful indeed, with the salt ponds in the middle and the many windmills turning gracefully in the breeze. The one main road was Victoria Street stretching from north to south with Balfour Town as the centre. There was hardly a time that we did not meet with friends and relatives when walking about day after day.

In the picture you can see most of the area that is Balfour Town stretching from the middle of the island going northward. The horse stable was in the yard where the two windows can be seen moving south on Victoria Street.

Fig. 3 -Victoria Street

Along Victoria Street you entered Balfour Town. There were a couple of little houses and a little shop down by the Anglican Church area, and there were always the two upstairs houses in the Balfour Town section: one a family home, and the other was the Brown House that was vacant and we considered haunted. As children we were afraid to go in the yard, but some of us did hide our sandals over the wall on our way to school and collect them on the way home.

Both the School and the Government Office were a little way up. This area was a bit scary for most children and adults especially at sundown because there was the Anglican churchyard with many graves, the haunted house, and further up was the Benevolent little house near the road with a hearse inside that we were afraid to look at because we knew that it was used to carry the dead. After sitting and hearing superstitious stories from the older folks that made children very much afraid to walk this area when it was dark.

Houses were whitewashed, while some had mild colours looking so beautiful amongst the oleander, hibiscus, bougainvillea, lilies, tulips, yellow elder plants, and all the other green trees that made the scenery of the community beautiful.

Fig. 4 - Old House - *Here you can see the back design of an old house showing the adjacent washroom. The clothesline posts are recent.*

There is also another road at the eastern part of Salt Cay known as Bleakly Highway that was cleared during the tenure of Commissioner Mr. P. Bleakly, but the natives referred to it as the "new road." Folks used this road occasionally along with another broad footpath known as the embankment that was adjacent near the main pond. Whenever we walked this path we would often see iguanas running across; they were very popular in Salt Cay at that time.

THE LIGHTHOUSE

Salt Cay also had a Lighthouse that was very beneficial to sailors travelling in Turks Island waters at night. They could navigate and avoid the shoals and reefs as the little light shone from this lighthouse guiding many boats and ships as they were passing near the island. This Lighthouse was probably built in the 1940's and during my early years, I could remember Mr. Albert Williams my uncle (aka Al Boner) the keeper making sure that the lantern was lit at sundown and shining brightly through the window giving light to those at sea. As time moved along the navigational operations improved and a battery-powered flashing light replaced the lantern.

There were steps inside the building that took you to the top and you could look out of the little window and get a good view of the Island and all the little Cays nearby. The Lighthouse was on the Bluff Hill located just at the western peak. It's the same point that all boats come around "the bluff" as they approach Salt Cay. Children had fun when there were picnics on the hill and we were allowed to go inside the lighthouse and look around. Sometimes we had to go over this hill and down into the bush to gather bundles of sticks and chop wood for the coal-kiln, but we always went on further to the bay area to pick grapes, caucus plums, or even look for almonds and coconuts that sometimes could be found while gathering sea-grass for the coal-kiln.

A True Little Lighthouse Story

One Christmastime, when Uncle Al Boner was keeper of the lighthouse he decided to secure his ham that he had received from his relative in New York by hanging it in the lighthouse. Unfortunately a group of young men, knowing that it was there, went one night and robbed him of it. Since the door was locked, it is said that they stood on one another's shoulders in order to reach the little window to get the ham. The next morning as Uncle was on his way to the lighthouse to put out the light, he noticed something strange – a dog with a hambone.

Right away he figured that something must have gone wrong so he hastened his steps to the lighthouse all to find out that his ham was really gone and that was his hambone.

During those days we made songs about every or any-thing that happened, so this time was no exception, so we went ahead and added a verse to Steal 'em Sam as follows:

> Steal 'em, Sam, Steal 'em Sam
> Steal 'em, Sam, the rocky
> Somebody steal Al Boner's ham

O ham, Boner's ham
No black people's mouth won't eat my ham
O ham – Boner's ham

(See ring games song at the back)

Fig. 5 -The Lighthouse on Bluff Hill

CHAPTER 3

THE SALT INDUSTRY

The Salt Industry started in Turks Islands as far back as 1744, and in the 1900's it was booming in Salt Cay and was the only kind of work that brought income and revenue for most of the people living there.

The first settlers were the Bermudians who came to work the salt; they originated from the African slave trade and they left ancestral family surnames like Smith, Taylor, Williams, Lightbourne, Simmons, and Forbes just to name a few. In 1951 the private owners sold all salt ponds and equipment that were used in the making or shipping of salt to a Government-controlled liability company known as Turks Islands Salt Company, TISCO. The early settlers constructed many places of interest one of which is the White House. Lots of salt was stored in the basement of this building as well as under the Morgans' house in the South District and also on the bottom floor of the Brown House. There were at least three or four large salt houses on the island because much salt was being produced.

The Salt Industry

There was coarse and fishery salt shipped in bulk and the granulated salt was shipped in bags. The coarse salt was extracted from the ponds and left to dry in heaps, while the fishery salt was the type that was ground fine and used for curing fish. The granulated salt was only three-quarter ground as it would be used in the Tanning Industry in Jamaica when shipped. At the back of the White House there was a seaport Harriots' Dock where salt was loaded on the lighters in bags to be transported to the steamers. There was also a special part for bulk shipping at the dock where salt was glided into the barge or the lighters. In 1960 a pier was dredged and a loading chute built to aid in the shipping of salt. All the area surrounding the White House was allocated for the Salt Industry and was called Harriots' Place. Adjacent to the White House was a branch of the Turks Islands Salt Company, TISCO, and that is where most of the salt operations took place. The upstairs building seen in Fig.6 was the Administrative Office where all the paperwork was finalized and all records kept.

The salt checkers did not sit in the office all day; they had to be out in the sun walking along the trenches and on the deposit sites to check the loads of salt carried and how many men were working for the specific hours daily. The names of the labourers and their time score, records of payroll, names of the ships that came for salt, along with the recorded amount of salt that was shipped daily, had to be processed in the office as a weekly report. There were only about three men working in the office and no female secretary.

In one of the buildings there was a machine to grind salt. My daddy was one of the operators and one day as they did some maintenance, he shouted, "I got it! " Half of a finger was cut off and it bled profusely as he took the long journey by boat to Grand Turk to see the doctor.

Fig. 6 -The White House and TISCO buildings. *You can see windmills, salt ponds, and trenches.*

HOW SALT WAS PROCESSED

Let me share with you what I can remember about the process from my Primary School classes and with help from other sources. Salt was made from seawater with the help of the sun and wind. First a canal and ponds were built, and this

The Salt Industry

was done by the first settlers who came from Bermuda, who also constructed water wheels and windmills to work the salt as far back as the 1700s. Water came from the sea through the canal that is in the North District flowing into the main pond, which was quite large. After the impurities had settled, the water was pumped by windmills into a number of smaller reservoirs, the ponds that were separated by stone trenches that had little openings for the water to pass through. As time went by, the sun evaporated some of the water. That which remained would become stronger in saltiness, turning to a pinkish colour, and was called ***brine***.

There were pond keepers whose duty it was to see that the canal doors were opened and closed at the right times and seasons to keep the water flowing right and have the windmills turning during the process. Mr. Welly Been and Mr. Albert Smith always kept busy at this, along with my father who also repaired both the windmills and the sails in company with Mr. Felix Lightbourne and other men who knew just how to handle them. The sails of the windmills were of hard cream-colour material, fastened to the wooden frames and strong enough to endure any type of weather. (See See Fig.7)

Fig. 7 - An Old Windmill

The pond keeper was responsible to test the water to know when it was strong enough to be pumped from the main pond to all the remaining ponds, which was done by the windmills turning day and night. This brine was then left until salt was formed with the help of the sun. This process usually took about six months. When the ponds were sparkling with lovely white crystals and no more pinkish water could be seen, the salt was ready to be raked.

The Salt Industry

Fig. 8 - Men raking salt to be transported to the heap.

When the salt was ready to be raked, the manual-labouring process began. With the use of pick-axes and rakes, the men would work the salt from the pond and shovel it into mule carts. Later during the time of the Salt Industry, the tractor and steam shovel were brought in, making labour less burdensome; then later still a truck was provided to transport the salt from the ponds. At this time the horses and carts were quite worn and not able to hold out much longer.

As men worked in the ponds, most of them would be barefoot standing in the brine and salt for hours. Why brine? Brine would surface as the salt was picked and raked, depending on the depth of the salt, so this was quite a labourious task for men working in the sun. A few of them wore water boots or cowhide sandals to protect their feet. They all wore straw hats or some sort of head protection as shade from the heat. The salt was deposited in heaps on the specially prepared area where it was left to drain and dry before being stored in the salt houses.

There were heaps and heaps of salt deposited in both the North and South Districts, looking like Crystal Mountains glittering in the sun. It was our delight to climb the heaps and pick pieces of shiny salt to take to school and at home. Oh yes, we ate salt as if it was candy, especially with green tamarinds.

Fig. 9 - Men carting salt to the heap as the foreman looks on.

Since there were docks and salt deposits in both the North and South District, the salt was transported from the docks by the lighters out to the ship that was anchored in front of Salt Cay. In the north there was Deane's Dock and in the south Harriot's Dock and Dunscombe Point. Some of this salt was also ground fine in a salt-mill and packed in bags for shipping. Bags of salt were loaded into the lighters and transported to the ships.

Fig. 10 - Salt lighters anchored at Deane's dock, north district.

Most of these boats were built by James Been, Norman Talbot, Clarence and Samuel Simmons, and others who were excellent boat builders and carpenters, and some of these men owned these boats. They sometimes got assistance from boat builders in the Caicos Islands.

These men made their canoes and used these boats to earn their living.

Sometimes both men and women would help to bag the salt as they worked from the salt house. It was during these times when men and women came from the other islands, especially Grand Turk, to work in the industry. Salt bags were made from a special type of material by the women who were paid to stitch them on machines. Salt was transported to the ships in the salt lighters and later by the barge and stored in the *hold*. About 6 or 8 men worked in each lighter as a team to get the job done. Crane buckets or dippers were used to take the salt from the boats to be stored on the ship. Salt was shipped to America and Jamaica and Europe and money and other produce were given in exchange. The Salt Industry was carried on for many years before coming to an end in the mid 1970's, but the last shipment of salt was made from Salt Cay in the mid 1980's according to records.

Fig. 11 - Food was kept hot in the carriers.

When men were boating salt, the mothers would prepare meals to send to the men. Food was placed in carriers, along with a glass bottle of hot cocoa. These were usually placed in a cloth bag or basket for protection because if not, many children got in trouble by dropping the bottle and spilling the cocoa, leaving the father with nothing hot to drink all day.

WHALING

There was another little industry that was worked in Salt Cay; this was "Whaling." There was a season when whales were being watched as they swam in our waters and came to the surface to breathe. The whale hunters were called Whalers, and they would go out in their specially built boats with strong ropes and harpoons so they could catch one or two to bring to shore. Whaling was somewhat dangerous; therefore, the boats had to be handled skillfully. One end of the rope would be tied to the boat and the other to the harpoon. Harpoons were hurled at the whales to strike them just below the shoulders to weaken them. I understood from the many tales told by grandparents that they had to be struck several times to make them weak because it was only after they were weakened enough that they were towed to shore or else they dragged the boats for long distances away from shore. Tales were also told of boats being carried as far as the Dominican Republic and some boats were overturned when the men had near escapes from drowning. When the whales were finally brought to shore, they were killed and taken to the Whaling Station that was at Whale House Bay situated on the eastern shores of Salt Cay just in the back of

Taylors Hill. The meat of the Humpback whales and Finback whales was good to eat, while the Sperm whales were hunted mostly for their blubber or fat that could be found under the skin on the whale's back and in its belly. It was boiled at Whale House Bay in great big iron pots producing hundreds of gallons of oil. When the oil cooled it was poured in drums and bottles and shipped to Canada and other countries where it was used for making soap, sperm candles, margarine, and other products. Eventually the whales stopped frequenting our waters in schools and this industry came to an end in the 1960's. Whale-watching season still continues in Salt Cay and is very exciting. **Whale House Bay** is one of our historical sites where you can find the remains of whalebones and an old tank at the location.

The highest point at the east of the island is Taylors Hill just above the plantation area. At the top of this hill once stood the remains of a big building, which is believed to have been the home of the plantation owners. The Bermudian slaves that were brought in on sloops to make the salt pans had another big task of cutting down trees and planting and harvesting guinea corn for food for both themselves and their animals. Most of these slaves lived on the plantation, except for those that worked at their masters' homes. They used horses, donkeys, and carts for all their transportation and labour needs.

The Salt Industry

Fig. 12 - Before the twenty-first century the Turks Head Cactus grew wild in Salt Cay.

CHAPTER 4

OUR HOMES – OUR ABODES

In Salt Cay nearly every family had a home of their own. There was no renting of houses. Most buildings of the 1800's and early 1900's were built with Bermudian stone with the walls in some cases being fifteen to twenty inches thick. The windows had so much inner space that we sat in them as if on a chair or sofa. Some houses were built of large stones that were gathered from areas around the island. The mason would shape these with his rock hammer and axe. Some houses were also made of wood. Large pieces of wood and beams could be found on the bay or seashore, called "drift wood," and most folks got this wood to assist in building. Wooden houses were sometimes made in one area then pulled on wheels to another as the family desired. The roofs of the houses were of some material called roofing, wooden shingles or zinc, and one could even see a few houses with the thatched roof and bamboo or bay reeds for the housetop.

Bay reeds are round long pieces of wood that drifted on the bay usually at the back of the island. The doors and windows of the houses were wooden shutters hung on the outside with hinges, and a few houses had inner windows and doors made with small wooden blinds or mesh wire screens, but say nothing about the cloths used in windows that had a string at the top and bottom. At night all outside shutters were tightly closed with an inside hook, latch, or wooden bar. Now, this was not for security reasons but for protection from rain or insects since every house didn't have inner doors or screens.

When folks left their homes to go elsewhere, whether day or night, they secured their doors with small padlocks, while others would just turn a bent nail or a small wooden bolt across their doors and windows. The insides of these houses were very beautiful; the floors and partitions were made of wood. In rare cases some rooms were separated with beams and cardboard. The inside of some houses was often painted, but the cardboard partitions were usually decorated with paper from fashion magazines that was pasted on. This paste was usually made of flour and water. A bit of kerosene oil was put in to keep the rats and roaches from having a meal on the partitions. The majority of houses were whitewashed on the outside with "lime." You may ask where did they get the lime? Lime kilns were made from conch shells, and of course there were lots of them. The shells were burned similar to the coal kiln, but the shells turned powdery. This powdery substance was put in buckets mixed with water and allowed to set until it became thick like paint. Some water was added and the mixture was used to whitewash houses. Some people would even put a little colour in this mixture because this gave the houses a beautiful appearance. Most houses consisted of bedrooms, a dining room, a kitchen, and the hall. The *"hall"* was a small room in the house that was well decorated and only used to entertain special visitors or guests. This little room had chairs that were carpenter made and nicely varnished or painted to match the interior of the room. There was a table covered with a pretty fabric or plastic tablecloth, and beautiful cushions were made for the chairs, not to mention the scrap-mat so very colourful and attractive that was placed in front of the door on the inside. Some homeowners gathered a fresh bouquet of flowers to put on the hall table every Sunday. This was normally placed aside the kerosene lamp having an attractive shade with the words "Home Sweet Home," and pretty curtains were hanging at the door and window.

There were no elegant bathrooms with the bathtub, toilet, basin, or shower, but there would be some sort of washroom in the yard or joined to the house for bathing and washing purposes. They had wooden tubs cut from barrels or aluminum and galvanized ones. These were brought in from overseas on the freight boats or from Haiti, along with beautiful enamel basins that could be seen in every home. In some homes you could find beautiful bathroom accessories in sets consisting of a basin, a ewer (big jug) a pail, and a soap dish. These would either be of enamel or very thick china (antique). Every home had a potty, a pail, or slop bucket that was used in the bedrooms at night apart from the toilet in the yard.

Some bedrooms had antique furniture that comprised a mahogany chest of drawers, along with a mahogany frame, or perhaps a frame of cast iron. These beds had a very soft mattress that was usually brought in by the husband who was sailing to the United States, Holland, or other foreign country. Most bed frames were constructed by local carpenters, having strong wooden base and legs; the mattresses were of very thick cloth and filled with grass that was normally pulled from the yards and left to dry over a period of time.

The bedrooms looked exceptionally beautiful when the beds were draped with "a piece coverlet"; this was a patchwork bedspread made of many small pieces of pretty cloth, usually by hand or stitched on the sewing machine. In Fig.13 below, I've tried to show what the things looked like that we used. The basin is what's left of a bathroom set that my mother displayed quite neatly in her bedroom.

Fig. 13 - Here is an enamel basin from a set, a tub and a piece coverlet that we used in early times.

The tubs were used for washing clothes and bathing purposes.

In the rest of the house there was a table and one or two benches, a cupboard for food stuff that was made against the wall, and a little fancy cupboard made of wood and mesh wire with some paint or dark varnish; this was called a "safe" and all the china and glasswares were kept in it. Some of those wares can still be found in my home and other homes today.

Where there were very large families and insufficient beds, parents would spread crocus sacks on the floor with a brown-cotton sheet for the children to sleep on. We didn't have blow-up beds nor small mattresses.

Pillows were also made of brown-cotton material stuffed with cotton or down, usually brought up from the Caicos Islands; some women would have the children cut very small pieces of cloth to stuff the pillows and this was very painstaking. In every yard there was a pit latrine or outhouse. In my day we said "the closet," not even the toilet. We kept them very clean – in fact they were scrubbed and washed down every weekend.

For lighting facilities, every house used kerosene lamps with glass shades or some folks had kerosene lanterns, and perhaps some had a can-lamp with a wick bearing a flickering flame without a shade; therefore, kerosene oil and matches could always be found in homes.

Flashlights were quite common in those days, too, and they were used when going out on the streets in the nights or in dark places in the house and around the yard.

One of my uncles had a flashlight that could hold about six D cell batteries.

The churches moved from kerosene lamps to *tilley lamps* that operated with mentholated spirits having a pump that made the lighting very bright. In the mid 1970's they began using private generators. It was around this time that two families began to own generators also and the island began to transition. The day finally came in 1980 when some houses were wired, a power generator was rolling, and electricity was turned on in Salt Cay through Turks and Caicos Utilities Ltd, Grand Turk.

Every family had some sort of kitchen that formed part of the house or there was a hut or caboose. In this kitchen there was a fire hearth, a brick, or box oven and a table (the dresser) with a dish pan to wash the dishes and pots. Food was cooked in strong iron pots either on wood in the fireplace or on the coals stove. Children went in the bush and gathered bundles of dry sticks to be used in the fire hearth; we had to chop tree branches and stumps that were not so dry that could last a while under the pots as the food cooked. For cooking, the pots and kettles were placed on the blazing fire that our mothers would kindle with oil and matches and sticks. When the food was being cooked, the wood sometimes gave off lots of smoke, especially if it was not dry enough, but the food would be delicious when finished.

Fig. 14 - Cooking delicious food

The Coal Kiln

Burning coal was not an easy task. Tree stumps and green acacia wood were chopped and burned to make coals. To make the coal kiln we cleared a patch of ground, digging a little below the surface, laid plenty of dry sticks on the ground, then placed the other wood on it in layer; we would put sea grass on top and all around and cover it all over with lots of sand, leaving an opening to throw in some kerosene oil, and light it. When there was a good blaze inside, we covered the hole with sand and sea-grass, leaving it until all the wood had burned to coals, which took about three to four hours depending on the size. If these kilns were not timed and watched, they could burn to ashes. Some kilns were left burning overnight if they were very big and this was because some folks sold coal by kettles and bucket measures. When the kilns were opened there was no more wood or fire, black coals were taken out and spread on the ground, smothered with lots of sand to cool. When the coal was ready, it was used in an open stove or in the box-oven.

Some ovens looked like big wooden boxes lined inside with tin, while others were of bricks. Both types of ovens were used with a coal-stove usually made from a half canister. Bread, cakes, gingerbread, cupcakes, bread pudding, cream cakes, and every other kind of sweet bread was baked nicely in these ovens. Johnny cakes were mostly baked in pots with coals on top on a piece of tin and fire under the bottom. Every woman in Salt Cay did her own baking. Here is a recipe that came from Mrs. Emily Hamilton's Kitchen.

Aunt Ella's bread recipe

Ingredients:
3 lbs. flour
4ozs lard/shortening
⅓ lb. sugar
1pk. yeast
½ teaspoon salt

Mix a pack of yeast with a cup of water and let stand for 10 minutes. It will rise. Combine this with all other ingredients in a large bowl, mix it with your hand, adding only enough water to make a thick mixture; knead (on a board if desired) into a light dough. Let rise for an hour or two. Put the dough on the board and cut into pieces, roll these into loaves to fit into 3 one-loaf greased pans. Let the loaves rise again. Preheat oven to 350; place in oven to bake for 35 minutes or until brown.

Remove from oven and let cool in pans or place loaves on a cloth on the table. Bread can be cut in slices while warm and eaten with butter, jam, or as is.

CHAPTER 5

PRECIOUS PROVISIONS

FOODS

In the early 1900's food commodities were not in much variety but people were able to produce their peas, sweet potatoes, corn, pumpkins, and tomatoes in their yards.

Nearly every yard had a coop with hens, chickens, and roosters. The hens laid lots of eggs in the coop or in a nest, sometimes under a tree, in a neighbour's yard or in a pear-bush or thorny patch away from home and difficult to access. It was then she got a chance to hatch her eggs and one day you see her and a brood of chickens come home to the yard sometimes with about ten or twelve little chicks. When the eggs were collected, our mothers would put them in a large pan or dish with bay sand just turning them day after day. In this way they could keep dozens of eggs for weeks to use and sell. Hens and roosters were cared for and at some time or other would be killed for food. People also kept cows, goats, and pigs and raised them for food.

When the cows had calves, they would come to the owners' yards. They went in and out occasionally until the calves had grown and it was time to go back to the hills and get familiar with wildlife. Each calf was kept home in the cow-pen while the mother went in and out to graze on the grass and other greens, sometimes at evening and returning in the morning. At home she was fed with bran food, some special leaves, and given water enabling her to have good fresh milk to give every morning. I had the experience of milking our cows a few times and it was real funny. Many families had fresh cow milk every morning and enough to sell. Most people would often boil the milk while others drank it straight from the cow. Animals were killed for special times of celebrations or festive occasions.

Seafoods were common for us in Salt Cay, especially those of us whose fathers were fishermen. We enjoyed turtles and turtle eggs, conchs, crawfish, whelks, and even whale meat during the whaling season. There was always much scale fish including sprats that were fried dry and tasty. Mothers prepared hashed shark, tuna, and sometimes it would be salmon, kingfish, grouper, or barracuda. Red or black snapper, turbot, blue fish, white fish, hinds, conies, and hogfish were our regular fish dishes. Usually there would be so much fish around that people would preserve it with salt then hang it in the sun to dry as corned fish. Conchs were also bruised and hung outside to dry to be used at a later day.

People had a few vegetables growing in their yards and they were often sufficient to provide meals for the family. Boats came from the Caicos Islands and brought provisions such as peas, grits, corn, corn-flour, dried-conchs, sapodillas, sugar apples, hats, brooms, baskets, and any other produce that they could sell to our people, thus earning money for their livelihood. Our folks were happy for these goodies, especially those who did not grow any crops. Corn was bought and ground in the hand mill as some families produced their own grits and corn flour. The grits made delicious hominy or even peas and hominy and the corn-flour was used for meal bread and porridge which we called our "meal pap." Corn meal was bought and used to make meal bread and meal hominy. I can recall mother boiling it, then pouring extra dry meal to stiffen the hominy, and this is still a tasty dish served with steamed fish or even with scrambled eggs and sausage.

Let me excite you about the native dishes that were usually served at various meal times:

For **breakfast** we ate very tasty cereals like cornmeal porridge, cocoa-n-rice, cocoa or flour pap, rice-n-milk, oatmeal and barley, or some delicious chocolate lumps and these foods were sweetened with condensed milk most of the time. There were other breakfast meals such as fry-cakes, delicious homemade bread eaten with butter, margarine, or a piece of cheese. We had lots of eggs and they helped to complete any meal. We would also have yellow grits hominy or some johnny-cake with steamed fish. Once in a while we would be served boiled dumplings, sliced and served with syrup for breakfast or lunch. This was called **duff**."

For **lunch** we had just a catch-up; that's if we went home during school lunch hour. We would usually get a piece of bread or maybe some leftovers from breakfast and some sugar n water. If a Haitian boat had anchored that week, our parents would have lots of mangoes, oranges, avocados that were bought by the buckets and they would hang the bunch of green bananas and plantains on a beam in the top of the house with a sack on them to ripen.

Dinner in the afternoon was usually peas and rice, white rice, stew peas, peas and hominy, peas soup with dumplings and slippries, made with red peas, split peas or lima beans, any bean and pear bush soup. There was buds and rice, conch stew, conch and rice, pumpkin and rice, callaloo and rice. The meat cooked with dinner varied accordingly, so we could always look forward to enjoying some salt pork or salt beef in the food and some smoked herring, mackerel, and codfish hashed or steamed as the relish. Dried conch and corned fish came in handy with some meals also. Sometimes there would be steamed conch, fish, or turtle, or maybe some hashed lobster, turbot, or shark. Seafood was very popular for meals and our mothers knew how to prepare those dishes in every style.

Sometimes we would have avocados or plantains from the Haitian boat to help with the meals. Even though these describe our regular food dishes, there were days when our parents would have some bread baked or some rice or sweet potatoes from the ground already cooked and awaiting the father or neighbourhood fisherman to bring something from his catch to complete the meal (this was called "pen-on"), meaning they were depending on what might be brought in to complete the meal. At night we got a piece of bread or some hard tack biscuits and some tea. There was another seasonal delicacy that we were fond of. Men went to Cotton Cay or Little Sand Cay and brought back dozens of bird eggs and turtle eggs. Mothers would boil some of these while some were sold, but we had a feast on them. Sometimes they even brought lots of big grapes. Things and laws have really changed, and I must share sympathy with you who never had the chance to enjoy such natural luxuries.

HOW DID WE GET OUR FOOD

Food was imported to Grand Turk by Turks Islands Importers Company Ltd. (TIMCO) for The CRISSONS and other wholesale businesspersons. This food was purchased by our local storekeepers and other families, then transported to Salt Cay. The sailboats would go to Grand Turk for food, sometimes taking four to six hours to get there if the wind was not favourable. These boats had names associated with traditional families such as Shirley Queen, Belvue, The Julia, Northern Star, Bertha B, and Winifred B. In the early 60's they began using motor boats the Periwinkle and the Kent. They were bigger and faster boats used to pull a small barge or one of the salt lighters. This was added transportation that could carry folks to Grand Turk and return in the afternoon without spending so many long hours at sea. It was now much easier to obtain food and other necessities from Grand Turk for shopkeepers and members of the community. Drums of kerosene oil were bought to be sold in the shops by the bottles. As children we would go on errands to the food shops on foot whether in the North or South District. Sometimes we took shortcuts walking the pond trenches. I can recall catching a ride on the back of the lorry in the mornings when I had to go to the shops in the south district and get back home in time to reach school for 10 o'clock. The rides used to be fun.

THE MONEY WE SPENT

During the early years of my life we spent British and Jamaican denominations of pounds, shillings, and pence (£.s .d). Apart from shopkeepers getting food supplies from Grand Turk, there were a few families that could afford to buy food in large quantities and this helped to alleviate food shortages in the island, especially when the weather was bad and the boats were unable to venture from shore. When buying food from the shops, our mothers often gave us a note or a shopping list, along with a straw basket and little containers. What were the containers for? Dear readers, we needed those for the various food items like rice, lard, sugar, and flour that were bought in small quantities. There were no plastic bags or paper bags at the shops so we had to take containers for the food items that were weighed in the scales in pounds (lbs) and ounces (ozs) or measured in quarts, pints, and gills. If an item was priced at **5s . 9d** that meant five shillings and nine-pence.

On the shopping list when you read it in our dialect, it sounded like this:

For 1½d you say penny-hapenny
For 2d you say toup-pence (two pence)

For 3d you say throp-pence
For 6d you say sixpence and there was also
the farthing ¼

By the way, if you have any older folks around that lived in Salt Cay during those years, they can help you with the currency language and also help with the shopping list that follows.

A TYPICAL SHOPPING LIST WOULD LOOK LIKE THIS

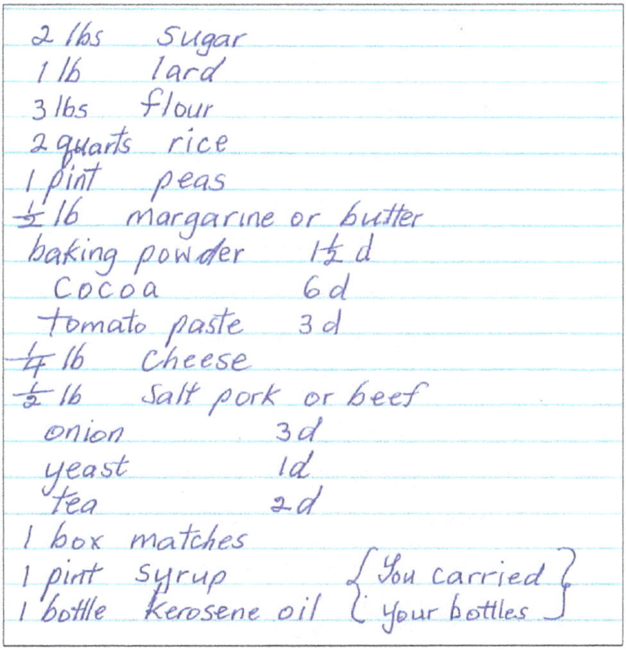

```
2 lbs    sugar
1 lb     lard
3 lbs    flour
2 quarts rice
1 pint   peas
½ lb     margarine or butter
baking powder      1½ d
cocoa              6 d
tomato paste       3 d
¼ lb     cheese
½ lb     salt pork or beef
onion              3 d
yeast              1 d
tea                2 d
1 box matches
1 pint syrup         { You carried }
1 bottle kerosene oil { your bottles }
```

Fig. 15 - Shopping List

Items like tea, cocoa, yeast, baking powder, and baking soda were sold in little cone-shaped wrappers prepared by shopkeepers to hold a certain amount. All I can say they knew what they were doing and had it together. Sugar usually came from abroad, packed in 100-pound bags made with layers of paper and plastic. The shopkeepers would pour it in large barrels then use the paper to wrap salt pork, salt beef, pig tail, mackerel, smoke-herrings, and codfish, also cheese and other foods that needed wrapping. Some of this paper was also used in the scales to weigh lard, margarine, and butter. Flour was shipped in 100-pound cloth bags and rice in sacks.

WATER

Our water supply was from government public tanks and wells. Water was sold for ½d a gallon. Some folks had a tank in their yards and gutters around the house to catch rainwater, while others had large drums and a single gutter. Guttering was not as sophisticated as the ones used now; they were made from tin or bay-reeds but they did a good job at catching water. For most families, water was transported to their homes by donkey and cart carrying a drum or barrel of water but usually by individuals who would tote buckets and canisters of water on their heads daily from the public tanks to their homes and sometimes from a good distance. There were times when we would even tote water from the school tank during recess (lunch) or after dismissal. Some folks had wells in their yards but this water was not so fresh. Those who needed some of this water from a friend or neighbour only had to ask and they were allowed to tote a bucket or more depending on how much water was springing in the well. This water was used for scrubbing floors and even for washing certain materials. There were two fresh water wells in the bush area at the north eastern section of the island, namely *front well* and *back well* and one in the southern section, *south well*. This water was also used for washing, bathing, cleaning, and even cooking, especially when the rainy season was slow and water was scarce. During times of drought, water had to be brought to Salt Cay by a barge from Grand Turk and sometimes from the Dominican Republic. When Turks Islands suffered a period of drought from 1956 to 1959, the m/v Kirknell came from Jamaica for a cargo of salt and brought in sufficient water in its ballast tanks for Salt Cay. There were times when water was rationed to families who only got two gallons a person for a week. A bit tough but it worked because the folks knew how to make a little bit of anything multiply.

Fig. 16 - Native toting water. We would tote water from near and far.

Most homes had a large clay jar sitting in a stand. These jars would be filled with water and one could get a cool drink at any time. We had no refrigerators or cold sodas, juices, or ice so these jars were very valuable and highly appreciated. Special dippers were made to get water from these jars. They were made from milk cans having long handles. Making these dippers was "a trade" so they were sold in the community.

Sometime in the 60's, a few persons began using kerosene refrigerators and deep freezers and now kool-aid blocks, and cold kool-aid became an exciting sale for some homemakers. People were now making ice in containers and it was time for making homemade ice cream in the hand-turning freezers. Not much meat was being frozen at this time. The kerosene refrigerator had to be given careful attention in order for the flame to burn blue and just right or there would be lots of black smoke coming from the back pipe and they didn't work well and nothing would be cold or frozen. Those things were something else. There was a big container at the bottom with rollers that one could pull out in order to put the kerosene oil in. You had to light the wick and fit the little shade properly before you roll it under again. This is the way it was before electricity was installed in Salt Cay in the 80's. At one time there was an underground cable in the sea from Grand Turk to Salt Cay but caused problems before the power plant was in place.

OUR CLOTHES

The clothing worn in the 50's and 60's differed much from those of the 80's and 90's. Nearly every piece of clothing that the majority of the people in Salt Cay wore was made on the island. There was a hand or foot machine in many homes and we had great seamstresses, but whether the women were seamstress of not, they made curtains, sheets, pillowcases, pillows, cushions, towels, and tablecloths. Every piece of clothing that we needed was made at home on the machine or by hand for the entire family. Clothing was made from different materials such as taffeta, silk, satin, voile, nylon, linen, and organdy but mainly of brown cotton, broadcloth, prints, and florals. Men's and boys' pants were made from corduroy and khaki. This material was sold in the dry good shops and measured by the yardstick. The women knew how to put a style or two together; they even made clothing from salt bags, flour bags, and gingham fabric. I can remember that there was a kind of material called "ticking" that they stitched together, leaving just an opening in the middle to put grass in to make the bed. Pillows were also made from this material. The seamstresses were versatile and dedicated. They designed and sewed clothes for babies, their shirts, the napkins, bands, dresses, and whatever, and the christening attires that they made were quite fashionable with the little bonnets and booties to match. These women even made dresses for the bride and her bridesmaids, and the shirts for the groom and his groomsmen. Only the suits were made in Grand Turk if needed because sometimes it was just shirt, pants, and tie.

Some of us got lots of clothing from abroad by parcel post. This was an exciting time for receiving jackets and sweaters, dresses, pants, shirts, shoes, sandals, and much-needed goodies. This was our bang-yang, and folks sold or gave some to their neighbours. People in Salt Cay looked forward to those big boxes coming by ships from relatives and friends living in America; that meant a different style of clothing.

All clothes were washed in the tub by hand or by using a scrub-board. Clothes were spread on any tree or on the walls to dry. These were walls built to secure boundaries of properties. Some folks didn't have a wall and certainly there weren't any clothes lines or dryers, so they would spread clothes on the grass or just anywhere. Sometimes it would rain as expected, and the clothes got a good beating and even got damaged or soiled when left outside for so long to dry. We had *surf* detergent, along with blue and brown washing soap, and there were some blocks of blue used to rinse the white clothes. The women would boil starch for certain pieces of clothes, so they would put them out to dry again in preparation for ironing. This was another task when they would sprinkle all the starched clothes with water, then roll them for an hour or so that they would be damp and ready for the hot goose ironing. Coals were set ablaze in the iron and allowed to get real hot; then all clothes were neatly pleated, creased, and smoothed, looking better than some garments that you can receive from the dry cleaners today. Most of the clothes were folded and placed in drawers or in a trunk.

HANDCRAFT SKILLS

Besides making clothes, the women did handcrafts like embroidery, knitting, and crotchet, as they made sweaters, caps, and socks for babies. Crocheted tablecloths, centrepieces, and lots of embroidery patterns were designed on dish towels and pillowcases also. Many of these pieces were for family use as well as for sale and gifts. The ladies did hem-stitching, downing, and smocking using ric-rac, lace, and ribbon, which tells that there was much for women to do and I challenge women of today not to let your cultural talents die; pass them on to the younger generation. The piece-coverlet was a patchwork made from six-inch pieces of colourful cloth and the scrap-mats were made from six-inch strips of cloth using a nail to punch it on a piece of crocus sack. It was in the early 70's that I learned to make punch rugs with wool, sack, and a punch needle, but I only got as far as teaching my girl, Whelma, but we made a few for special gifts. They were beautiful with patterns of three or four colours of wool. These mats were like the throw rugs of today; you would find them in front of the beds and door inside the house looking very pretty.

I can still lay hand on one of the needles, so I think I will put punch rugs on my next retirement plan and try passing that skill on. I have to say "next" because writing this book was my first plan and I've finally gotten there.

Fig. 17 - A sewing machine meant prosperity for any family.

CHAPTER 6

SIMPLISTIC JOY AND SERENE PEACE

CHILDHOOD DAYS – A BANG

When babies were born during my childhood days, there was a district nurse who visited the homes for the delivery. We were made to think that the babies were brought to the house in the nurse's big straw basket that she would bring with her. I suppose that was a part of our primitive ignorance since we had enough eyes to see Mama's stomach looking big, but we just couldn't ask too many questions of that nature or even talk about this to adults like our boys and girls do today. Mothers who were ready for delivery, whether day or night, would send their husbands or relative or even a friend on foot, on a bicycle or maybe in a donkey cart to call the nurse. There is a knock on the nurse's door and a voice: "This me…(name)…. My wife say come; she think she ready."

The nurse knew what that meant because the expecting mother had attended her clinics, so she had that big basket packed with all her necessary medical stuff awaiting the call. The nurse, along with the person, would hurry along; sometimes the basket was carried ahead as she took time to dress then followed on foot, depending on the distance. I shared some of these experiences because I often slept at her house. During the night when very late she sometimes took me with her, especially when the man went ahead on a bicycle and left her to walk alone. If the homes were not in walking distance the man came rattling over rocks and weeds to take her on the journey to the patient in the donkey cart, having a little lantern onboard. The nurse lived in the North District, so when she had to go south they usually travelled the back road, the new road, which seemed shorter.

After the delivery of the babies, mothers stayed in their warm and cozy beds for about nine days with rooms tightly closed, having only a flicker of a light from a kerosene lamp that had to burn very low. In those days babies were born with their eyes tightly closed, opening them gradually over a matter of days. The nurse made frequent visits for the first week or two to ensure proper care and good health for both mother and baby. When the mothers were able to enjoy the world outside their bedrooms it would be another three weeks of wearing shoes and socks, a sweater, and head tied with a scarf, and they were not allowed to move about too much. Haven't we come from a long way? These were the days when mothers would breastfeed their babies for a year, but they also fed them Lactogen in bottles and later some barley or corn meal cereal was added. Babies and small children were also given dill-seed and lemon grass tea to help the gas pains, and every now and then, some brazen bush leaf in water for cooling as they grew strong and healthy.

It was a wonderful experience having enjoyed good childhood years and later still as adults to live in the same neighbourhood and environment of our parents. Some children had the privilege of living in the same houses that their grandparents once occupied. I am proud of my heritage and feel highly honoured having lived in my parents' house, along with my children for a few years before relocating. I have a fairly good knowledge of what life had to offer from the early 1900's until the early1980's as I take a backward look.

Childhood Activities

In Salt Cay children played games and had fun with other neighbourhood boys and girls. We played and sang ring-games. Words to titles below can be found in the back of this book, along with a few actions:

a. There's a Brown Girl in the Ring
b. Steal 'em Sam the Rocky
c. Go Round and Round the Valley
d. All the Soldiers Marching Through
e. A Hunting We Will Go
f. Sugar You Come
g. First Time I Play With Trash
h. I Sat This Young Lady Down to Sleep
i. Round the Green Apple Tree
j. Billy, Billy, Hold Fast My Gold Ring
k. Puss in the Corner

We would also play games of hopscotch, bat and ball, rounders, (that was baseball), hide and seek, skipping, and other rhythmic activities. We also enjoyed playing jacks and ball using small rocks or any small objects with a little ball. At school we used the seeds from the cedar trees that we call bumpies. We also tried hula-hoop using the bicycle wheel when all the spokes were removed. Most of these games were played by both boys and girls.

Boys On the Run

Boys had their special times playing games of marbles and bat and ball as they practised cricket. Older men and big brothers helped to make little boats with sails on them that they would sail in the ponds. They also showed them how to construct kites that looked beautiful flying high in the sky during the kite season. Boys enjoyed spinning tops that were made by men of the community, rolling rims of old bicycle wheels for hoops, and making funny little slingshots with leather and small pieces of wire; these were the activities that boys enjoyed even through early teen years.

Girls Having Fun

As expected the girls played with dolls and dolly houses indoors and under the spreading trees. We would make our dolly houses, make doll clothes, have doll weddings, and play cook using our little play pots and tea sets. When we didn't have dolly pot sets we used tin can and old discarded bowls that our moms gave us. There were children who had no dolls, so when mangoes were in town the dry seeds were much appreciated as some little girls used them as their imitation dollies. They would wrap a piece of cloth around the seed for clothes and the long hairy part was considered the head.

Occasionally when moonlight nights came around, neighbourhood children gathered in the road closest to their homes to have fun playing games, singing, and running around. When it was time to go in at about 8 p.m. our feet would be so muddy and dirty – yes muddy and dirty until the mud was squeaking between our toes because we played barefoot. When playtime was over for the evening we would go to the neighbour who had a well in the yard and dip water to wash our legs and feet and return home to get a cleanup for bedtime. As children we didn't have much homework, neither did we have television, so we spent our leisure outdoors most of the time. As mentioned earlier, we had fun going in the bush to pick grapes and other little fruits, and besides we would go in the sea quite often, especially during summer holidays. We sometimes walked the beach gathering shells, maybe sea grass for the coal kiln, or to take bay sand home to sprinkle in the caboose or in front of the doors. We would also use this time to gather sea fans (huskers) that were used to scrub the floors.

Many of our fathers would be sailing on Dutch boats to Amsterdam-Holland and to North America with the National Bulk Company and to other European countries in the early years, so they would be away from their families for maybe nine months to a year and then return. This was a usual venture as fathers wanted to earn a good living for their families, and the families of that day were large, having mother, father, and eight or perhaps ten or more children. My family consisted of mother, father, and seven children so it was tough for many people to get ends to meet. Even when my father retired from sailing, he worked hard in the salt industry and in the fishing boat, making sure that his family needs were met. He also found it necessary to remain at home to help my mother to discipline us as we grew older and needed both parents as we matured. Most children, along with some adults, made a little money by beating rocks and selling them by the buckets. This only started when people began mixing concrete to build houses.

Usually when our fathers returned for a vacation they brought lots of housewares, clothes, toys, and other niceties so these families were considered well-off folks in those days, and their children were the ones who had the overseas goodies to show off amongst their friends.

There was a special time when girls from south and north gathered to have grand doll weddings at the salt shed near Deane's dock on Saturday afternoons. Family and friends came to support us. We would have a bridal party of different types of dolls and our little ceremony planned. Some dolls came from America dressed as brides, but adults made special doll clothes for us, and even made cloth dolls. After the wedding we served little pieces of cookie and other sweets, celebrating until sunset or until moon began to shine.

We often held our own neighbourhood entertainments in the afternoons, especially when school was on holidays. We would gather at a home singing and saying nursery rhymes like Georgie Porgie, Hey Diddle Diddle, and such. We usually met at a house where there was a piano, organ, or guitar and some adult would play music as we danced around making our afternoons enjoyable. Of course there was no television with cartoons to watch and our mothers didn't have jobs; therefore, they had time to get involved in our childhood activities, which we see very little of today. We also played games and had story time and drama directed by adults. All of these activities were fun and enjoyment for us to pass time.

CHAPTER 7

ENTERTAINMENT AND AMUSEMENTS

Amusements were very simple. All secular programmes were referred to as entertainments and the spiritual ones were concerts. Practices were always held for groups of persons whether young or old for whatever occasion. They would learn both secular and folk songs and special dance rhythms. Performances were also poetic and dramatic when both ladies and gents wore costumes and did much playacting. Special nights were set aside for the entertainments, especially Friday evenings, and by way of announcements a notice board was carried around from house to house by the Bell Boy who rang the bell throughout the community and at your door. When the door was opened he showed the board to be read and then went on his way.

The notice on the billboard read as follows:

STOP! LOOK! LISTEN!

THERE WILL BE AN ENTERTAINMENT HELD AT ST. JOHN'S SUNDAY SCHOOL HALL ON FRIDAY NIGHT STARTING AT 6 O'CLOCK

Entertainment and Amusements

ADMISSION:
Adults : 6 PENCE.....
Children : 1 PENNY.....

CREAM-CAKES, CUP-CAKES, FUDGE, DULCE, PEANUTS, PEANUT BRITTLE, and GINGER BEER WILL BE ON SALE.

If it was a concert notice the wording would differ slightly as they did not sell at the concerts. Churches usually had concerts on Sunday afternoons and they were well attended. Children and adults alike would recite and sing for any and every celebration, be it Christmas, Easter, or Mother's Day events. Concerts were only held in the evenings if in connection with a church Missionary Service or when the schoolchildren were having special plays for Christmas or Easter. Sometimes the Benevolent Society would have concerts in order to raise funds to help with much-needed expenses that they incurred from time to time like after the death of a member or for their anniversary celebrations. The Women's Federation would also put on entertainments to raise money to purchase materials and help with the Christmas party for the children.

These were the kinds of public outings all of us enjoyed in Salt Cay. When entertainments were held, various musical instruments were used and the participants or performing groups dressed in the prettiest apparels that one's eyes could behold. The music consisted of an accordion, a box guitar, maracas (shakers), a harmonica, and sometimes even a comb wrapped in tinsel played by mouth, along with the jazz horn that Mr. Traff played skillfully and melodiously. These instruments brought forth sweet musical sounds. Songs like "Brown Skin Gal Stay Home," "How Much for that Doggie in the window?" and "Raise Your Skirts and Show Your Pretty Knees" were sung and dramatized as the crowd would applaud and yell "Encore!" You would see dance steps like the shatee, ballerina, waltz, limbo, peppermint twist, heel n toe, and even the mash potato performed on stage and at dances.

There was no song so sentimental as "Dear John." A lady would sing this song to a man; during this performance it would be as though a hush was in the room. *It went thus:*

Dear John, how I hate to write
Dear John, I am telling you tonight
All my love for you is gone and it's for another one
Bringing back the same old message –Dear John

Many of the folk songs were very dramatic, like "Hit Him in the Head with the Frying Pan"; the ladies would carry specially made frying pans as they danced on stage with their male partners, and when they sang that part they would dance to the men and hit them on the head. It was fun and brought much laughter. The women sometimes dressed in men's clothing wearing a hat or cap. We could always look forward to Alf to make sport at these gatherings as he entertained the crowd with his favourite song. He would often go on stage with a bunch of flowers and sing, "I bring to you this big bouquet of roses, one for every time you break my heart," and he would throw flowers across the stage as he did all sorts of body movements and unfamiliar facial expressions that we called the "monkey face." He was a real comedian filling our days with much laughter and fun *right down inside of Salt Cay*. Italicized words borrowed from my Headmistress Ms. Mary Robinson.

Often times the plays were exciting and very enjoyable. The curtain was fixed so that it could be pulled across for each performance as the audience waited with great anticipation. The adults would practise children to take part in entertainments and concerts as well, so we had our nights to perform every now and then and we were also among the groups when they took their entertainment performances to Grand Turk. At this time they would take along all the homemade goodies where they would make money and draw a crowd.

Fig. 18 - This is our comedian of the day…Alf
(aka Brake)

PICNICS

Holidays were picnic times when families and friends gathered in an open area where they could find trees to give shade; this was usually in the north bush area known as Front Well or on Taylors Hill in the eastern section of the island. Sometimes we would go down Bluff Hill according to the occasion, a church outing, or just children's picnic. When we went on family picnics, they loaded the stuff in the donkey cart, or in most cases everybody took something to carry on head or in hand and went picnicking. Folks carried food stuff, water, pots, and other goodies. Everybody had to carry their enamel plate, spoon, and cup because there was nothing disposable around. Our mothers set up some stones to put the pots on while we gathered the wood for the fire. They cooked different pots of food under the trees, tasting and sharing meals and sweets as they talked and interacted with each other. Wherever these picnics were held, we had fun running through the little trees searching for crab holes and looking to find some of our little bush fruits. Sometimes the older folks told us stories or taught us some tricky games to make the day enjoyable. At sundown we all returned to our homes.

Here is Aunt Vida's Candy Recipe

2lbs white sugar
1½ cups water
2 teaspoons vinegar
1 small bottle peppermint

Combine sugar, water, and vinegar in a medium pot and allow to boil until you see very big bubbles. Put a small stick or knife in the pot and lift it out; you should see a thick thread dripping. You need to have a piece of marble or a big tray well greased to pour this mixture on. It will be hot but use your hands to keep folding it over for a couple of minutes.

If you want to mix a colour you divide the candy mixture in 2 pieces; then pour peppermint in one piece, and peppermint and some food colour (red) in the other piece. Fold the pieces separately; then begin pulling to produce the candy. Pull and stretch it wide, bringing the ends together as you continue pulling. When it starts to get hard and look like candy, put the 2 pieces together and pull and twist them. You can break the stretch in smaller pieces as it will get longer and you'll need to pull these pieces to the candy size. Now you use a knife and cut up the colourful stretch into small candies. By now they will still be a little warm, so keep shuffling them on the tray so they wouldn't stick together, and sprinkle them with some sugar.

Now you can share these with family and friends; you can even sell some. She or someone in her family can also make a candy basket for you. Just ask.

GARDEN PARTIES

These were fun times usually organized by the churches for fund raising. People gathered to meet and chat and especially to buy and sell, as each of these functions would have lots of fudge, milk-dulce, coconut-dulce, candies, cream cakes, cup cakes, peanuts, and peanut brittle. There was also ginger beer and lemonade sold by the cupfuls. These parties were well supported and attended, and both children and teens played ring games for most of the afternoon and well into the evening.

The **Baptists** held the **Mayfair** where plaiting the Maypole and climbing the Greasy Pole were the highlights, especially for the youths. For the Maypole there were long colourful strips of cloth hanging from the top of the pole that was usually planted in the yard for this occasion. The young people were taught how to plait it, moving over and under to create a beautiful pattern on the pole. Now the Greasy Pole was something else. The men would plaster it with thick, dark cartwheel grease. This had to be done before the pole was planted. Now the boys would put on old clothes and try to climb as high as they could; of course the pole was very slippery and greasy making it difficult for anyone to climb; therefore, people watched with great anticipation to see who would climb the highest. It was really exciting to watch these activities.

The **Methodists** would plan a **Valentine Party** every year with lots of assorted Valentine cards displayed to be sold and of course lots of sweets. A little Post Office would be set up in a corner of the Sunday school hall where this event was held. As cards were bought you could go over to the post where someone stamped the envelope using an ink pad; then some other persons were given the task of walking around trying to deliver them. The words of one popular Valentine card come to mind that read:

> "You pig, You hog, You dirty swine…
> I don't want you for my Valentine."

School girls and boys had fun sending these types of little cards to one another through the party post.

There were also cards with beautiful readings like "Roses are red…" and we found pleasure in sending them to our special friends.

The Anglican Church usually sponsored an **Easter Monday Fair**. Miss Mary Robinson co-ordinated this fair. She would have lots of Easter goodies and sweets on sale. There would be cakes and other special items for raffle and even had an Easter egg treasure hunt. This fair usually started from about noon and continued until night when there would be rip-saw music and dancing.

Now, there was always an expectancy for the closing of this function when about 10 o'clock she would stop the music, even while people were still wheeling their partners, and say, "Let us all stand and sing the QUEEN" (that meant the National Anthem), and everyone knew it was time to pick up their bags and sweaters to leave. You may say, "What a way to end a party" knowing that could never happen with twenty-first-century young people. Think about that.

OTHER CELEBRATIONS

Christmas celebrations were spectacular; there were many attractions with merry-making. Folks went all out as they do now. Houses were whitewashed in and out with a little colour to make them look beautiful. Doors, windows, tables, chairs, benches, partitions, and the safe were painted, varnished, or papered. We would go in the bush and chop a nice sticky bush tree to decorate with crepe paper, balloons, and ornaments made from cigarette and matchboxes with tinsel (foil) and Christmas paper. The Christmas tree was in the **hall** that was also decorated with flowers from the yard and a string of Christmas cards that were sent to the family. We often used that same dried sticky bush to sweep the yard, but during Christmas we got bay sand to sprinkle in front of the doors to give our surroundings a new look. All children looked forward to Christmas presents and shopping, the Santa Claus gifts under the tree, and a party or two. There was the usual Santa surprise from our parents on Christmas Eve night, but our gifts of the 50's and 60's varied much from what is being given now. Our Santa gifts were comprised of slates, pencils, a colourful enamel plate and mug set, a top, a ball, lots of sweets, and perhaps our pretty socks to wear on Christmas Day. Children who had relatives in America or fathers sailing for the Dutch or National Bulk companies got expensive presents like tricycles, dolls, trucks, little umbrellas, pretty school bags with their books and pencils, even apples, hard candies, and some nuts. Sometimes mothers even baked meal bread with raisins for gifts, especially for their teenage boys, and these gifts were greatly appreciated and enjoyed. I can recall one of my two brothers walking around with his loaf wrapped and holding it tightly under his arm just letting anybody know that he was not about sharing it. For Christmas presents people gave things like a handkerchief, a bottle of Khus-Khus, a comb, a tin of powder, a cake of soap, a belt, a pair of barrettes and socks, or a tea-set for little girls, while boys got their socks, some marbles, a jack-in-the-box, or a top. Although these gifts may seem quite simple now, they were of value during that time.

During the Christmas season, the Child's Welfare Association would have a party for all the babies and small children during which time gifts were presented to them, along with other goodies. The Women's Federation also gave a party for older children and dolls and trucks were among the gifts. There was always something special about Christmas celebrations. There would be serenading from house to house with Uncle Sammie playing the accordion and the rest of the ripsaw band having Alf beating the cow-hide drum, Mr. Will scraping an old saw with a big nail and Mr. Fee on the box guitar and folks singing songs like: "Ma Ma bake the Johnny cake Christmas comin...."; "Good Morning, Good Morning, how are you this morning?" along with many other folk songs that were usually composed by the men as they walked from house to house. As the musicians entered a yard, they would play and make up a song with words like this:

> "We wish you a Happy Christmas…
> I'm out in the dew, I'm soaking right through
> Sue please open your door
> You know what we lookin' for."

Families gathered in their yards or joined the crowd in the streets to dance and jump up as the ripsaw band played and crowds followed. There were many more men in the band but they often played at different times and places. When serenaders turned in at folks' doors, they were usually given some cake, pudding, some Ruby Red wine or Pear Wine or maybe some homestyle ginger beer. That's what they were really looking for according to the words of the song.

Processing Pear Wine

How was this special Pear Wine processed? Pears were plucked from the prickly pear bush tree. They were cleaned and cut then squeezed into a jug with a little water, then strained. More water and sugar would be added, along with some raisins, a little corn or rice, and some ginger. This liquid was poured in tightly sealed bottles and buried in the ground for about a week or ten days. During this time, the liquid became fermented from the heat, so when the bottles were taken up, you had real Christmas wine ready to share and enjoy. This is how we practise doing it, and one time I fell in the pear bush patch gathering pears to make my pear wine, and of course my aunt had a task picking the tiny prickles from my skin. Yes you can laugh; it was funny.

Homestyle Ginger Beer

Preparing ginger beer meant boiling some ginger and sweetening the liquid with sugar. Some rice was also put in it as you add water and let it remain still for a few days in a closed container. This liquid produced very strong ginger beer that families shared or even sold at parties.

Entertainment and Amusements

Dancing the DOLLBABY HOUSE

During the Christmas season it was our culture for men to dance the DOLLBABY HOUSE; this was usually the New Year's Day celebration. This event was a serenade of musical instruments with the same group that went throughout town on Christmas Day but there was more.
The leader Uncle Rody and his group would dance through the streets in both the north and south districts. He danced with a dollhouse on his head, while both young men wore masquerade faces made of cardboard, tar, paint, feathers, and whatever else to make it look scary as they would make funny sounds. They also wore old clothes decorated with paper, paint, and colourful strips of cloth or paper. The dollhouse was made out of cardboard and decorated with colourful paints, some feathers, and Christmas paper with a circle cut in the bottom to fit on the man's head. Everyone looked forward to these celebrations for Christmas and the New Year as they joined the crowd dancing through the streets making merry. That was our Christmas Masquerade performance every year.

A Special Christmas Service

Another highlight in Salt Cay for Christmas was attending a special Christmas Day Service held at the Anglican Church every year on the 25th of December whatever weekday except for Saturday. When it was Christmas Day, the majority of the folks got dressed in their newest and best, along with their children, and went to that 11 o'clock service. I know you may ask if this was during the daytime. Yes, in the burning heat of that special weekday but sometimes the rain did fall.

Other churches held their early morning Christmas Services at 5 a.m., but people from all churches attended the Christmas Day Service. This custom continued for a long time, and I must say amongst all the celebrations, this was one of the highlights of the season. All children looked forward to wearing their new clothes, shoes and socks, and some of us had hats and our little new umbrellas that we could use whether it was hot sun or pouring rain. The biggest disappointment for Christmas would be a downpour of rain and we couldn't go to church all dressed in our new clothes. The *joke* that cracked all over the preparation was this: while the church's second bell would be ringing (yes Anglicans used to ring first and second bells for every service) and the service would soon begin, some persons, especially children, would be almost dressed but awaiting a piece of clothing that would be still on the machine getting the finishing touch, or some parent would be just trying to clean the spots of paints off their skin using a little kerosene oil before leaving home, but nevertheless we all got there. During this season, children were taught to make chains from oleander leaves to decorate the churches. It truly was an exciting time.

CHRISTMAS EATS and DRINKS

At Christmas time a cow and a pig would usually be killed and folks throughout the community would buy the meat for their special dinner. Some families would even kill the yard rooster or hen and cook some nice peas and rice or stewed peas and white rice, serving it with steamed chicken, beef, or pork. Tasty dishes of meat such as these were only eaten during these festive seasons; therefore, we looked forward to enjoying our sumptuous Christmas dinners. We never really mentioned side dishes because some fried plantain or some vegetables from the ground made a normal meal at any time. Remember now these were the days when no refrigerators were in our homes or in any stores; therefore, meats were cooked and consumed daily or perhaps left in the pot for the next day with the hope that it would not spoil, and it usually never did. This was the time when cakes were baked for Christmas and every family would try boiling a pudding for the New Year to be served with some delicious sauce. Family and friends visited and celebrated as they ate and drank cake, pudding, pear wine, and homestyle ginger beer.

DANCES

On special occasions, dances were held in the nights, and the ripsaw band, along with music on those 45 and LP records, was played on the record players or on the old gramophone. We also knew about the record player that had a handle to wind up; that was the rectroller. The type of dancing was the shatee, waltz, also the limbo and peppermint twist, along with little slow movements.

Sometimes a musical group of young men would come over from Grand Turk to play music for weekend parties and dances. They were THE FLAMES comprising Lamuel Been, Vincent Wilson, and Charles Taylor originally from Salt Cay, and Vernon Ellis, Llewelyn Simons, and Preston Malcolm from Grand Turk. These guys displayed great talents as they sang and played the instruments skillfully.

CHAPTER 8

TRANSPORTATION and COMMUNICATION

BY LAND

I know we act as if we cannot walk long distances, but in those days there wasn't much transportation, only donkey carts and bicycles; therefore, walking was not a problem and we had no reason to complain. There was one car in Salt Cay owned by the **MORGANS** and we spoke about it as "the motor car," but my sisters and I got many evening rides in it. Besides that, there was a tractor, a lorry, and a loader the vehicles that were later brought in to advance the Salt Company. People did not feel the need for anything else since the donkey and cart or a bicycle was the only type of transportation that some families had, so everyone was accustomed to walking everywhere they had to or wanted to go. As children, we had fun going for family rides during moonlit nights in the donkey cart with our fathers or uncles. We would spread sacks or a piece coverlet in the cart and carry a little kerosene lantern. The donkey and cart was the only means of carrying loads of wood, drums of water, loads of rocks, food stuff from the boat, or any other heavy burdens. The only horse and cart that was used by a family was Wild Alice – a horse that used to chase us if we went too close, but she was tame with the owner, and his family enjoyed many rides as well. All other horses, mules, and carts were used to carry loads of salt from the salt ponds to make heaps or carry scales and mud from the old ponds to build up the roads.

The animals used for transportation were domestic animals and very tame. The horses that were used to cart salt were kept in the company horse stable in the south district, while owners kept their animals in a pen in the yard. This was done in order to give them the needed food and water; then they were allowed to roam the streets and any other places, but every tame animal knew the yard called *home*.

Fig. 19 - This background is a bit recent, but this picture depicts the way we looked as we enjoyed our evening rides with our fathers or uncles.

SEA

Many sailboats and canoes could be found tied to the shore or anchored off at Deane's Dock in the North District. These boats had names such as the Northern Star, Winifred B. Shirley Queen, and Belvue. They were about 20 to 24 feet long and were used for transporting people, food, and other commodities to and from Grand Turk on a weekly or even a daily basis. There were times when sick folks had to be taken to Grand Turk for emergency treatment. The boatmen and family members had to take the long sailing journey sometimes late at night with a lantern or flashlight, which took them two to three hours on the sea, in order to save the life of a loved one.

During those hours from Salt Cay the nine miles to Grand Turk seemed like forty-nine instead, and looking back at those circumstances, they were very pathetic and wearisome, but it always worked out good with God on their side. The men were very learned and skillful in navigating and making trips in the day; therefore, it was never a big problem for them during the night. The boats needed the wind to blow from the right direction in order for them to move ahead. There were days when the boat would leave Salt Cay dock from five in the morning and never arrive at the Grand Turk wharf until twelve noon, all because the wind was light or too calm; therefore, the boat just had to beat and tack to reach the shore. In other words, the winds were contrary to their sailing. This was a bit tough but necessary if our people were to get some food to cook, some kerosene for our lamps, or some materials to make clothing, and even to get the sick to the doctor. All of this, along with other pressing needs, gave the boatmen courage to keep on, and more so because these journeys were part of their daily living for wages.

There are numerous stories of boats being caught in bad weather and the perils at sea, yet this was the only way at that time. It was not until the mid 1960's that boats with motors began operating to and from Salt Cay. The Government had a motor boat, the KENT, sent from South Caicos, that would journey between Grand Turk and Salt Cay, transporting passengers and sometimes towing a small barge or a lighter (sailboat) in order to carry food and other necessities, including water to Salt Cay when there was a drought.

Sometime in the 60's another motor boat was brought in from Jamaica; this one was repaired and named the PERIWINKLE, perhaps because lots of periwinkles could be seen on the drift wood and found around the rocks near the seashore; they resembled whelks but much smaller. So there was no name more fitting for the boat. Men usually gathered periwinkles for fishing bait, but the fame on that name is that we were usually called, The Salt Cay Periwinkles. Whenever the inhabitants of Salt Cay could put foot on Grand Turk and walk the streets, we could hear sounding in our ears, "Look at *The Salt Cay Periwinkles!*" and we embraced that name for years without fear or shame.

AIR

The first time a plane landed in Salt Cay was sometime in 1966 when a pilot named Fritz Ludington came in with a one-engine plane and landed on the east road in the vicinity of the ponds near the airport. That day the Head-teacher and everyone ran outside, filled with excitement. Afterward another one-engine plane began coming in from Caicos on private visits. In 1967 Lou Winnery started making a few regular flights in his 5-seat Cessna and air traffic took off from then.

There was really no airport there, so the little planes landed on the same parcel of land with weeds and stones that was later reconstructed into an airstrip by the Government. A shelter was built and daily flights began operating with Air Caicos. Our first airfare was just $4.00 roundtrip to Grand Turk and we landed on a part of the Prison Folly in the area near the Bible Baptist Church because at that time no other planes were allowed to use the airport at Pan-Am Base; it was private property.

Here is a funny tale about Brake, our comedian. One day the plane came to Salt Cay to take passengers to Grand Turk and Brake wanted to make the trip over but he only had a dollar. Those were the years when pilots collected the money as you boarded; there were no ticket agents, especially when there was no airport or building.

He gave the pilot the money and said, "Mr. Pilot, I only have this dollar so you can drop me halfway." It was funny but the pilot was used to his jokes so he smiled and took him on.

It was the years when Brother Fred Carlson, Brother Jack Harvey, and other missionaries began visiting Salt Cay in their little plane. They brought "Chuckles" and "Uncle Cousins," two puppets that sang and dramatized as the missionaries conducted services quite often at our school. These missionaries conducted Bible study sessions and taught us many choruses. The community was really uplifted spiritually.

COMMUNICATION

The only form of public communication in Salt Cay during the early years was the VHF wireless telegram system through Cable & Wireless in Grand Turk and the Government Office VHF Radio. To send a message from Grand Turk to Salt Cay, one had to go to the Cable & Wireless Office and deliver the handwritten message to be sent, and in Salt Cay the messages were sent to Grand Turk by wireless. There were messenger boys who were paid to go around delivering the notes received. This was especially necessary when a loved one was sick or had died. If there was news from overseas during the hurricane season, folks would gather outside the Government Office to hear the latest news that was transmitted by wireless. It was the duty of the Government Officer to relay all information to residents.

In the late 50's about two or three radios were in Salt Cay, owned by families of fathers or husbands who were travelling abroad and had the opportunity to purchase one. The Government had a News Bulletin read on the radio at 11 a.m. courtesy of Cable & Wireless Messrs to share

Transportation and Communication

information to all of the Turks and Caicos Islands. I can remember hearing the call-in buzzer sounding throughout the neighbourhood from the radio as adults hurried to get near the walls of the houses in order to listen to the news.

Later on a few more folks got radios and people began sending messages to persons on other islands through this medium, and one could now get information much quicker, but it first had to be sent through the Office. Handwritten messages were taken to Cable & Wireless in Grand Turk to be read on the news bulletin for a relative on another island; for example, "To Joy Brown in Salt Cay, I am sending you a box on Wednesday; let me know when you get it." There was nothing private about this; everyone could hear once they were tuned in, but it was helpful because someone could relay the message if the other person didn't hear it.

When this operation first began some folks did not understand what it was all about, so it is said that a man in Grand Turk once loaded his donkey cart with a bag of flour, a bag of rice, and a canister of lard and went to Cable &Wireless hoping to send those items to his family on another island. He didn't know what was really going on. Haven't we come from a mighty long way?

A little later we became listeners of the Gospel Station 4VEH from Cape Haitian, Haiti, that was transmitting loud and clear. People began sending song requests and greetings to 4VEH to be read for loved ones and friends. That was when we learnt songs like "Across the Bridge," "My God is Real," "Life is Like a Mountain Railroad," and other lovely gospel songs. On 4VEH we began listening to *The Children's Bible Hour with Uncle Charlie and Aunt Bertha* with the children singing lovely choruses and Aunt B would tell those heartfelt stories.

Folks began to learn many songs for concerts and other spiritual gatherings. This radio station revived our spirits for many years. As time moved along some people began to pick up a station or two from America and listen to Billy Graham, Back to the Bible Broadcast, and the Gospel Bells program from Nassau, Bahamas. Those days were great, and people began corresponding with preachers overseas, and now the Government postal service was being utilized more often.

MAIL

Mail was transported on the sloops that were used to trade dried conchs and other goods to Haiti and the Dominican Republic. Some folks sent their mail direct to the 4VEH station when they knew friends who were travelling to Haiti. Other routes were surface mail through Jamaica by the m/v Kirksons and Kirkland and airmail through Bahamas. Letters, cards, big and small parcels from America and elsewhere usually came by surface mail. When the mail arrived in Grand Turk, it was sorted and sent on to Salt Cay by boat. Folks who had parcels would sign a slip and pay a fee in order to collect their goods. This is still a way of making revenue for the Government, but it was the only way to go at that time. Package mail from the Bahamas was usually done by the Caicos boats that journeyed on that route as a means of livelihood for the boatmen who transported passengers, food stuff, and other goods.

THE PRINTED PAGE

Advancing into modern communication, Salt Cay began receiving news bulletins during the early 1960's. We had *The Pelican*, which was produced voluntarily by Government staff as a weekly paper, then *The Torch*, a paper published by the Grand Turk School Literary Society. *The Conch News*, published by John Houseman, carried lots of news and even encouraged gossip because people were now reading or hearing some interesting happenings about the islands, which sparked wall-to-wall and door-to-door conversations. Most of all, the people had a better understanding of what was going on in the Turks and Caicos Islands.

The Government had its own form of paper news; this was the Gazette, which was done by the Printing Office. This paper contained news of local interest informing of Government happenings, politics, and legislation, along with our little foreign news letting us know what was going on in other countries that we were connected with. The Gazette would also tell when a new Administrator or Governor was coming to Turks and Caicos or leaving, and who other dignitaries would be visiting from where and when.

CHAPTER 9

RELIGION AND CHURCH ACTIVITIES

In this chapter, I will share with you the Religious aspects of our island during my early days. From my childhood there was always St. John's Anglican Church, Methodist Church, and Mt. Zion Baptist, and everyone knew what it was to go to a church service on Sunday.

As I grew so did the churches, and a branch of the Church of God of Prophecy was established in 1967. The usual Sunday morning services were held at 11 o'clock by all churches, it was Sunday School at 3 p.m., then the Evening Service. Monday was prayer meeting night for Baptists and Methodists, and the Anglicans had usual Wednesday Evensong. The Lenten Season was observed and on Ash Wednesday the Anglican Church conducted a service at 11 a.m. During this time, almost every child and teacher from the Elementary School would attend and adults took time from whatever they were doing to attend also. The Church of God of Prophecy held regular services weekly, along with revivals and District Conventions; therefore, it is safe to say that all families could choose the type of religious or spiritual background they desired for worship.

Many of the special events that churches celebrate now, such as Mother's Day and Father's Day with concerts, were the usual, along with Christmas and Easter programmes with plays, recitations, singing, and musical selections. Events like these brought much enjoyment and fulfillment to the lives of the people, encouraging them to understand the life and love of the Lord. In a later chapter, I share more about Congregational Gatherings and Services held in the community.

Christening, confirmation, water baptism, weddings, and funerals were ceremonies conducted in the churches, but not with as much grandeur as seen now.

FUNERALS

Funerals were conducted for all the dead by a church no matter who you were. No corpse was carried directly from the house to the graveyard; the body would pass through a church for a service before burial. Most people died in their homes, and funerals were held within 24 hours of a death. There were times when persons would die at the hospital in Grand Turk but their bodies could not be preserved since there were no morgues in those days, so the dead had to be buried as quickly as possible.

MY SAD STORY

Here is a personal experience that I will now share with you. It was on December 16, 1968, in the peak of getting ready for Christmas when my father faced a tragic death by drowning. His funeral preparations and burial all took place within seven hours of our family receiving the news and I was the one to help my mother do all preparations since the older siblings were not on the island. I was so busy that I only came to grips with reality and mourned his loss when the body left the house for burial. As I look back, I can thank God that He made me to be strong through difficulties even then.

It happened overnight in Grand Turk at the south pier where my daddy was overseeing the boats that were tied to the wharf. These were the Salt Cay boat and barge that had to off load a freight ship and the sea was a bit rough. It was discovered early the next morning that he was missing and he probably had fallen overboard at night while checking the boats, so the scenario began. Divers had to go down and search the dock area for the body. It was discovered and taken to the hospital.

My family in Salt Cay was notified by wireless communication at about 10 a.m. Right away we had to begin making preparations. We lived north, so I got on my bicycle and went around notifying family and friends in both North and South Districts about the sad news. I had to inform the Benevolent Association because the Fraternity was responsible for his burial. They got the grave dug and a coffin was available; it only had to be given its finishing touch. While the plans were being carried out, a postmortem was being done on his body at the Grand Turk hospital. The cathecist was also notified.

In the meantime, family members were able to get a flight to Salt Cay for the funeral at 5 p.m. The body was eventually flown home about 3 o'clock that afternoon and brought to our house where it was prepared, dressed, and placed in the coffin *by a dear lady Ivy Smith who was a close friend of the family with assistance from others. People gathered at the house; we took our final look as a hymn was sung. They closed the coffin and walked in a procession behind a pickup truck that transported the body to the church. The funeral service was conducted, the burial took place in the church yard, and we returned home having done it all just before night fell.*

Wooden coffins of various adult sizes were usually made for members of the Benevolent Association and kept until needed, so that is why one was ready to be used for my daddy. When a child died, a carpenter had to make a coffin that same day or overnight, so if there was a light in the carpenter's shop during the long hours of the night and you could hear the saw cutting and the nailing of the hammer, you knew that a coffin was being made.

These coffins were lined inside with white cloth, having a tightly fitted cover and ardently varnished. In those days females were buried wearing a white shroud and the males had on dark suits or just a shirt and pants. Sometimes the dead would be placed in the coffin with some pretty flowers and the body was viewed at the home or at the Benevolent Hall, especially during the times when the hearse was used to transport the dead.

A funeral service was quite ordinary; there were no booklets, no, "As I knew him" or obituary, not even any special funeral arrangements. After the singing of a few hymns from the church hymnal, a scripture was read; prayers were said by the minister, who then read his sermon; and the corpse was taken to the burial site. Most Anglican members were buried in the church-yard, and this was the case of my father. Other burials took place either in the south or north burying ground, the Government cemetery.

Before there was any motor transportation the coffin was usually carried in a donkey cart or lifted by family members and friends to the church and also to the burying-ground. The Benevolent Association had their hearse that was pulled by a mule so it was more convenient for those who were members of that organization. At the time of my father's death, there was no more hearse and mule.

Traditionally, family members would mourn for their loved ones by wearing black, dark, or mild-coloured clothes for six months to a year, depending on the closeness of the relationship. They wore those dark clothes everywhere; they wouldn't let the children of the families wear bright colours.

If we did put on a piece of bright clothing a family member would say, "Go take that off; your aunty (or whoever) ain't been dead long enough yet." That tradition was rigid and some older folks are still holding to it strongly. Even though there were no wreaths and cards sent to the family, it was a tradition for family members to gather natural flowers and lilies as they prepared little bouquets to put on the graves of their loved ones. They would do this every Sunday until they were satisfied to stop.

WEDDINGS

Courtship, engagement, and marriage. How was it? Weddings were always enjoyable in Salt Cay. Leading up to the wedding day there was a time of engagement and courtship during which time the young man would visit the girl in the evening at her parents' house. This courtship time was referred to as "on the bench." Now this visit was checked by time.

If the gentleman came to the house at 7 p.m. he had to leave by 9 or you would hear one of the parents begin clearing the throat or close a window. They did something to get the young man's attention to let him know it was time to leave. Some mothers took the privilege to call the girl's name out loud and she knew what that meant. Somewhere during this period of courtship, the couple would plan their wedding. The attire for all the bridal party was usually made locally, except for persons who had relatives overseas that would send the bride's dress or some pretty fancy material.

In the early 1900's marriage *licenses* were issued from the Magistrate's Office in Grand Turk costing 5/ (five shillings) and I sometimes heard men saying "I only buy you for 5/." The ceremony was conducted in the same manner as far as the vows were concerned, and there was only one ring that the groom gave to his bride, and on some occasions that was borrowed from a relative and returned. There were no large bridal parties, no programs sheets, no bridal aisle runners, and no petal droppers. There would be about two or three bridesmaids and groomsmen and a flower girl walking behind the bride, carrying her pretty little basket of live flowers and usually holding the tail of the bride's dress.

We heard nothing about breakfast weddings, only afternoon weddings celebrated with lots of cake, Haitian sodas, wine, and rum. The bridal party had to walk to the church and to the reception, and it would be quite messy and muddy if it was rainy. The one car on the island was only for their family, but if the couple was special to them, they got a ride. At the reception, folks would just congratulate the bride and groom with hand shaking, hugs, and a few jokes, while the enjoyment of feasting and merrymaking was going on. It was the custom in those days for the bridal party to go to the Sunday morning service as a "turnout," especially if you got married on a Saturday. Sometimes the couple and attendants would get all dressed again in their bridal attire as they went to church and receive their first communion together. This was mostly an Anglican tradition. The young groom usually had his own little house ready to move in with his new bride and enjoy their lives together.

CHRISTENING and BAPTISM

This ceremony was done in all churches. Before babies were a year old they were taken to the house of God for their blessings. In those day the boys had two godfathers and one godmother, while the girls had two godmothers and one godfather. Now, there are so many god-parents at the font or altar during christening, that an explanation would need to be given to our fore-parents concerning their tradition.

CHAPTER 10

SCHOOL AND EDUCATION

In Salt Cay all children went to a preschool that was usually held in some older person's house. At about age six, we started going to the Public school. There was always that one Elementary School in Salt Cay, but we obtained a very good education. There was the Head teacher and five other teachers with an enrollment of over a hundred scholars when I attended.

The School was one main wooden structure during the earlier years; then in 1951, a stone annex was built on the western side, along with a catchment tank and a big platform since no gutters were affixed around the roof. Round about 1970, an Infant classroom was added on the northern side of the main building, giving the little ones more space now that free play activities were introduced and became mandatory by the Education Department. Our school system began with the small children being in Junior A and Junior B; from there we went to first standard and on to sixth standard year by year. The system ran this way until the 70's when we began with Kindergarten 1 and 2, continuing on to Grades 1 to 6 at Salt Cay Primary School. Education was the key at Salt Cay School and we were well taught by all our teachers because Miss Mary Robinson, who was the Head Mistress of the school for many years, assured that everything went according to the rules and the syllabus and that we did not waste any time. She was also the teacher for fifth and sixth grades during her tenure so she prepared us to write external examination, thus producing some of the most successful scholars in the Turks and Caicos Islands at that time.

Mr. Clifford Jones was the Schools' Inspector in the Turks and Caicos and he visited every school, giving written and oral tests every end of the school year based on subjects and lessons taught from the syllabus, and this school was no exception. Even though we didn't have anything written in books to study, we had it in our brains that served us like computers. Our memories were quick and sharp. I must make mention of my teachers; they were: Mrs. Eleanor Godet (nee Taylor), Mrs. Mary Stovel (nee Simmons), and Mr. Vincent Wilson (Picky), along with two very stern educators who were instrumental in propelling many boys and girls into their destiny during my day: Mr. Oswald Smith and Mrs. Eliza Simons, along with my private tutor, Mr. James Morgan. This school advanced academically, and was one of the best performing Elementary Schools in the Turks and Caicos Islands. We were taught from Jamaica Caribbean Readers that we could buy and take home, but the British or Jamaican Arithmetic books were used only by our teachers.

We had NO bags packed with textbooks. It was unusual for us to do much writing in books except for a few subject notes and writing compositions, and this was only for the upper standards. In second, third, and fourth standards, our teachers gave us sheets of paper for our writing practice and we used stick pens, jugs of ink, and blotting paper. We used slates and pencils even for homework so you could imagine us getting disciplined with that cedar stick when we entered the classroom and our work was all rubbed off the slate for whatever reason.

In the 60's, scholars were prepared at this school to write the First, Second, and Third Year Jamaica Local Examinations. A few of us even did Private Studies in preparation to write the London Chamber of Commerce (LCC) examinations also, of which we were able to be successful in a few subjects. Many children were fortunate to attend the Secondary School in Grand Turk, but some could not because of the low income that their parents earned, and boarding was not affordable. For those who attended the Secondary School, they received a boarding grant from the Government of £10 (pounds) and this was a good sum in those days.

Our school started at 10 o'clock; we had lunch hour from 1 o'clock, during which time most children went home to get a piece of bread or a fry-cake and some sweetened water, syrup and water, or switcher, or perhaps only some water. Switcher was sugar and water with some sour limes squeezed in it. We returned at 2 o'clock and our school day ended at 4:30 p.m. When it was time for school to begin, the timekeeper who worked next door at the Government Office would hoist a big black ball on the flag pole that was planted in a base at the entrance of the school grounds. This was to signify it was 10 o'clock and time for school to begin.

There was also a time when a bell in the office yard rang at 9 o'clock. This is because our school hours had changed and school ended at 4 o'clock. While we were on the road, we could see if the ball was going up or hear the bell ringing and knew that we were late. We began running even across the trenches, knowing that we just might meet the door closed and we would get flogged by the Headmistress, but it wasn't that way all the time.

We didn't wear uniforms and very few of us wore slippers or sandals; if we did they were either hand-me-downs or bought from the Haitian boat. For those of us who had footwear we didn't appreciate it; therefore, we would take them off and hide them behind some tree or throw them over the Brown House wall in Skipper Harriot's yard and collect them on our way home. We preferred going to school barefooted like our friends. Children living in the North District use to take a short cut by jumping over the canal doors and walking on the pond trenches, and sometimes this caused problems because when the doors were opened for salt-processing purposes, we would close them down so that we could jump across. Children from the south walked the folly or the south road while some took to the pond trenches for the short cut. Those of us whose fathers sailed to foreign countries had ready-made school bags, while the other children had handmade cloth bags or little straw baskets to take our slate, pencil, and reading book to school.

School and Education

We had to foot it to school and back twice a day whether it was rainy, windy, or sunny. Some of us wore Haitian straw hats and some girls would use their little Sunday umbrellas while the boys wore caps. This kept us from the heat of the day, and if you don't believe me, the sun was just as hot as it is now, I mean scorching hot. The roads were sandy or had scales from the ponds so our feet never had to endure the heat from asphalt.

School was fun and we enjoyed times of being assigned as helpers to do the cleaning. A "Duty List" would be posted every Monday morning, showing who would sweep the floor, wash the cups, and clean the latrines. This was for the entire school because we had our aluminum cups, a bucket of drinking water, and a basin with soap and water to wash our hands after using the latrine, which was a little out house with two separate parts for girls and boys. We enjoyed doing our chores at school regularly and daily. Every Friday we would clean the latrines with salt water and disinfectant using a broom, then sprinkle lots of bay sand on the floor.

We could do this because the school was near the beach, just as it is now, and sometimes we would even clean the cups on the bay. Once or twice a year the older students were responsible to see that every desk was scrubbed, including those of the little ones, so we had to bring our soap, old rag, and husker (sea-fan), along with some yard clothes, and get scrubbing. We even scrubbed the benches at times. A special afternoon was set aside for this and we looked forward to an afternoon break from the usual classroom routine. There weren't many public holidays for children to have a school getaway, so we spent many days at school and hard at work.

We were privileged to enjoy Easter, summer, and Christmas holidays, but they were not as long and at that time, our school's calendar was from January to December.

Fig. 20 - Salt Cay Primary School

As mentioned earlier, our school was comprised of one main wooden building with classes from Junior A up to fourth standard before the Infant block was added.

We had no dividers; the only thing between each class was the blackboard on an easel. I don't know how we did it, but the teachers taught us and we learned well. The fifth and sixth standards were taught by the Head teacher in the annex that can be seen in the picture between the main building and the tank. We did Extra-Curricular Activities like practising for concerts and plays, sewing, and other handcrafts, which were taught by volunteers, and we played games and did sports.

We even practised girls' netball with instructions from our Head teacher, who had brought that sport home from Shortwood Teachers' College, Jamaica, where she was trained. School Sports were held annually on the cricket field and sometimes on the school grounds. Our sports comprised most of the cultural events like skipping, running, three-legged race, egg and spoon, needle and thread, high jump, potato race, and even hula-hoop with bicycle rims.

We also had open races such as eating the bun without touching it as it hung from a string, and say nothing about the bicycle race when you got a prize for riding the slowest and getting to the finish line without falling off. These sports were lots of fun and excitement. We did not receive trophies or medals. The awards were neatly wrapped gifts consisting of a pack of marbles, a small compass, a cake of soap, a ball and paddle, a skipping rope, and perhaps socks and hair accessories, or even a doll, and you dare not tell us they were not gold medals because they were highly appreciated.

At one point between 1950's and 60's our school had distribution programmes of non-fat skimmed milk, cheese, butter, and UpJohn vitamins. Teachers prepared canisters of hot cocoa and served biscuits provided by funding agencies in the United Kingdom and United Nations. We were quite happy and blessed to have these foods; it made the day for many families. When Turks and Caicos had affiliations with Canada, our school had a link with a School in Canada as "Twin to Twin Schools"; therefore, we joined hands and hearts across the miles by communicating with letters and cards as pen-pals. We also had a few calypsos about our twinning relationship; the words can be found at the back of this book.

The school in Canada sent us lots of books for our school library, some clothing, and even some furniture, and in return we sent gifts of handcrafts and shell work. I recall that we even sang the Canadian National Anthem in our class at times. With no text books and very little notes in our little copy book, our brains had to be strong to remember what we were taught in order to write tests and examinations with success.

Salt Cay has produced some very intelligent men and women from this School and there are still many of them holding very prominent positions in Government and the Private Sector throughout the Turks and Caicos Islands and even abroad. If you would ask scholars like me, we'll tell you we never attended the Secondary School in Grand Turk, but were successful because of what we were taught at Salt Cay Elementary School. In 1963, I enrolled in a Typewriting Correspondence Course from Scranton, Pennsylvania, USA, and the success of this enabled me to teach typewriting to a few young girls at my home; they later migrated to Grand Turk and were appointed jobs in some Government Departments using that skill. Oh! Salt Cay was Great! And still is. If time has forgotten it, we can never. There are too many precious memories.

CHAPTER 11

CIVIC GROUPS AND ORGANIZATIONS

There were a few Civic Groups organized in Salt Cay during the early 1900's and most persons, especially children, were involved and played significant roles.

Girl Guides, Brownies, and Boy Scouts

"The First Turks Island Girl Guides Company" was established as early as the 1930's in Salt Cay by two of the Morgan Sisters on their return from Jamaica. It was fun attending meetings of Girl Guides every Monday afternoon at their residence. Growing along with this group were the Brownies that consisted of the little girls. "The Boy Scouts" never started until 1952 with Reverend Hugh Sherlock, a Methodist Minister from Jamaica. During his visits to Salt Cay, he, along with Mr. C. S. Jennings, the Government Officer, began gathering young boys on **The Hill**; that's The Government House and this movement began.

These movements had one goal, to train boys and girls to grow up with integrity and good morals. We were taught the Rules, the Promise, and the Motto, "Always Be Prepared." At these meetings we played our usual games, but when Lady Agar visited from Jamaica she taught us new songs and games. We learned to sing "White Coral Bells," "Insey, Winsey Spider," and Have You Ever Seen a Lassie," just to name a few. Girl Guides had to practise to tie various knots and do some basic first-aid training using bandages. Social graces involved making beds and setting tables. Sometimes we would go on picnics and be given cooking tips as we prepared little meals in the outdoors before having a test in the kitchen.

At times the Scouts went on weekend camps, learning to construct tents in the woods and to use their lanterns and flashlights at night. These were the experiences that they looked forward to enjoying. They gathered sticks to prepare food, even learning to light a fire without using kerosene oil or any type of fuel. These boys were trained to tie their knots and do their bandaging also. Most of these groups wore special uniforms and took part in events such as the Queen's Birthday Celebration on May 24th, Armistice Day (Poppy Sunday), and sometimes during official visits.

Benevolent Union Association

Another group that was very outstanding was the Benevolent Union Association, which began in the late 1800's and was reorganized as a Fraternity on 29 March, 1915. Their badge depicted Faith, Hope, and Love. This group had their own meeting hall, located due north of the school. Men and women about forty years old and over formed this organization. Usually they would meet bi-weekly on a Tuesday night to plan and discuss matters. The members paid weekly dues and whenever any of them got sick, the association aided the family and was responsible for providing a coffin, getting the grave dug, and seeing that the corpse was transported to the church and on to the burying ground when any member died. The "Benevolents" as they were called, had a hearse drawn by a horse that was used during funerals to transport the dead. They always had a couple of coffins prepared beforehand and kept in the meeting house overhead. Perhaps in rare cases they had to prepare a coffin, depending on the size of the body. The coffins were made with a slight oval shape and nicely lined with white cloth, having a glossy varnish finish, along with a matching cover.

Fig. 21 - The remains of the Benevolent Hall with an old coffin inside

The Benevolent Association always celebrated the day of its re-establishment on the 29th of March with a special service, a parade, and a banquet. To enhance this celebration Mr. Nat Selver's Brass Band was invited from Grand Turk, along with the preacher. This used to be a grand time in which all the inhabitants of Salt Cay looked forward to enjoying.

They sometimes met with delays or disappointments if there was bad weather and rough seas, and this would also mean disappointments for the ladies who would be waiting to collect some of their attires from Grand Turk. During the turn out of the celebration, the ladies wore everything white from head to toe, and the gentlemen wore black suits, white shirts, black shoes, and felt hats. They went all out for this joyous occasion. The members met at their "hall" and paraded to the designated church chosen for this occasion.

After the service, they formed a procession marching, dancing, and jumping in the streets until they got back to their hall where there were lots of delicious food, drinks, sweets, and cakes prepared and ready to be served. The Benevolent membership donated, and had concerts and other fund-raising activities so they could meet the expenses for this grand celebration and any other needs that would arise from time to time.

The Women's Federation

Another outstanding group was "The Women's Federation," established by Lady Higgins in 1970. She was the wife of one of the Governors from Jamaica. This group gathered and occupied themselves in handicrafts such as sewing, crochet, embroidery, downing, and the like. Everyone shared her talent with another, thus they were able to make piece coverlets, scrap-mats, centrepieces, and shell work for their homes and to use as gifts. The Federation was usually overseen by the Governor's wife, who acted as patron and appointed a leader to keep the group going during her absence. She visited occasionally and provided the much-needed funds and materials to keep the association running productively.

Child Welfare Association

This Association was found and funded by the Government in early 1960 to help meet the needs of babies and young children under six years old. Regular clinics were held when babies were vaccinated and weighed and skimmed milk and vitamins distributed to mothers. A Milk Scheme was also organized to distribute subsidized milk – SEMILKO – to young children at a small fee to help raise funds to assist the Medical Officer in purchasing toys and other goodies for the Christmas party.

CHAPTER 12

SPECIAL EVENTS

Church Activities

From my childhood days, many events stood out and were celebrated as yearly highlights in Salt Cay. As you've read in a previous chapter, it was Valentine's Day celebrated by the Methodists. The Anglicans nailed it for Easter Monday with lots of fun for the children, teens, and older folks, and the Baptists would let us enjoy the May Fair in style held in Aunt Hester's yard where people enjoyed plaiting of the maypole and other fun and games. Later on most functions were held at the Government House **The Hill** where there was a large party hall and lots of space for children to play games and run around outdoors. Yes, the Government Officer and his family lived there but they worked along with any congregation in order to make the functions grand.

The Queen's Birthday

The Queen's Official Birthday celebration was a very outstanding event for the community held on a Saturday, but the 24th of May was the public holiday. This was similar to the Queen's Official Birthday Parade that is now celebrated in June. Weeks before this celebration, the school children and civic groups would practise the march and royal salute, along with their items for the programme.

On that special day teachers, school children, Boy Scouts, Girl Guides, Brownies, the Special Constable, the Nurse, our Clergymen, and nearly everybody in the community assembled on the School grounds and paraded to the area known as Middle Beach (a section in the middle of the island). The Union Jack would be flying on the flag pole as the Government Officer, the head of the island, stood on the pedestal to take the "Royal Salute" as we all passed in honour of the official command "Eyes right!"

The celebration began with the march pass in honour of the Queen, but when the parade ended at the school grounds, everyone was seated inside the school to enjoy a programme that had been arranged by the Head-Mistress. The school children performed with recitals and patriotic songs such as "Britannia the Pride of the Ocean," "Three Cheers for the Red, White, and Blue," and "John Brown's Body." Together we always sang the three verses of the National Anthem, "God Save our Gracious Queen." Speeches were given by officials including the Head-Mistress. This was always a grand celebration for this historic occasion. For the closing there would be lots of eats and drinks to refresh everyone.

Fig. 22 - The base at Middle Beach

Remembrance Day

Another special event in Salt Cay was Remembrance Sunday or Armistice Day Service when persons in the community wore poppies and all congregations assembled at St. John's Anglican Church. A special reading, "Let us now praise famous men...." would always be read, and a special poem was done by the school children entitled, "In Flounders Field the Poppies Grow..." These were some of the words we heard as we paid tribute, remembering persons who lost their lives in the wars, and saluted the others who were yet alive.

Parents, teachers, school children, Boy Scouts, Girl Guides, and Brownies would gather on the school grounds and parade to the church for this service. No wreaths were laid, but during the weekend a few Guides and school children sold lots of poppies going from house to house. Since this was a once-a-year event nearly everybody bought a poppy to wear for that Sunday.

A Time For Cricket

In Salt Cay there was a time when we all looked forward to seeing the cricket teams come in from Grand Turk and East Harbour-South Caicos. Great matches were played on the cricket field in the South District and there would be a party evening of appreciation. Later a small building was erected on the field grounds, "The Club House" thereby encouraging more recreational activities, and folks were able to sell goods and even food in their gatherings.

Guy Fawkes Celebration

Everybody in Salt Cay looked forward to celebrating the 5th of November. Our teachers told us about Guy Fawkes and the Gunpowder Plot that led to him being burnt at the stake. I don't know how far back this observance goes, but as children this historic day was high on our calendar of events. The weeks before this day, an adult leader from the north and south would gather groups of children and make plans for us to meet special afternoons to gather bushes and to choose boys who would make and wear masks.

We prepared a large heap of dry and not-so-dry bushes to make a bonfire for that night. In preparation for this event, some fathers and younger boys made fireballs from rope yarn and soaked them in diesel or kerosene for a few days so that they could burn well and last long when lit. The fireballs had wire in the centre with a long piece extended to hold and twirl around in the air.

We had firecrackers and thunderbolts, and on that night the boys would always put a firecracker or two in the middle of their fireballs to create excitement. Some of us would throw firecrackers in the air or even on the heels of each other. Fathers got some tar, feathers, paint, and cardboard and assisted the young men in preparing for their masquerade show. Mothers and the young women made effigies of Guy Fawkes for that evening and everything was ready.

Families prepared fudge, milk dulce, candies, and other refreshments to make the night enjoyable as we played ring games and danced around with guitar tunes. Both groups in the north and south gathered near the pond area away from all houses, but neither group wanted to be the first to light their bushes; therefore, we sometimes ran into nine o'clock just waiting. When the heap was finally set ablaze, the fireballs were lit and the masked faces came around making funny noises, causing the little ones to run and be afraid. At the end every Guy Fawkes was thrown into the fire and burnt.

Salt Cay Day

This event first began in 1978 when a Methodist group was camping in Salt Cay at the Brown House. They had many attractions planned for the closing day, which was a Saturday.

This included sports, a donkey and cart dress-up contest, and a gospel concert in the evening. A baby show based on healthy looks was also held at the school and I can remember my four-month-old son lying there smiling and winning the first prize. With so many activities planned for that day, it was decided, "Let's call this ***Salt Cay Day***," and it continued.

During that time only a few places had electricity, including the Brown House, so for the concert a stage was erected in the pond across the street and electric cords were used, giving a beautiful scene in the pond while the Methodist Choir and other singers performed, making the event a memorable one. Salt Cay Day continued to expand, becoming more secular as the Government took over, adding the beauty contest, other cultural activities, and dancing. People began coming in from all the family islands by boat and plane to celebrate until this event came to a halt perhaps after Hurricane Ike in 2008.

CHAPTER 13

VERY IMPORTANT PEOPLE and PLACES

Hello! What do you think? Yes there were Very Important People – V.I.P's in Salt Cay and I will make mention of a few who over the years helped to make this island a little paradise. The Government had a representative as the head of the island. He had the title of "***Government Officer.***" He either came alone or with his family, usually from Grand Turk, and he lived at the Government House 'The Hill' in the South District on the road to the creek. He wore many hats in that position being responsible for all Government undertakings on the island. He had to see that all jobs were executed daily and at the end of the workweek he was the paymaster. In his office was the Bank Treasury from which he paid all the TISCO workers, the teachers, the nurse, the district constable, and others who were apprentice workers.

Other persons and the local associations and churches used this Treasury to open savings accounts. As time passed, customers closed their accounts and moved to the Government Saving Bank or to Barclay's Bank in Grand Turk.

The Postal Service and all other means of communication transacted from this office. One could buy a postage stamp, send a telegram, mail cards and letters, or carry out any form of mailing service. Parcels, along with all other mails, were transported by sea and received at this office. Boats from Haiti and ships from Jamaica or elsewhere that came for salt arrived and departed under the Government Officer's jurisdiction; therefore, it could be said that he dealt with customs and immigration of the day.

In the South District on the road to the creek was the "Government House." Government Officers and their families occupied this house when they were sent from Grand Turk to serve their tenure. Some of them were Mr. Alexander Adams, Mr. Ulrich Williams, Mr. Alexis Williams, Mr. Robert Quant and Mr. Lloyd Been of Salt Cay who lived in his own home. The house began deteriorating and Government Officers ceased occupying it. The title then changed and those who served as **District Commissioners** were: Sterlin Garland, Stanley Brooks, Stephen Smith, Kingsley Been, Patricia Simmons, Lorlean Malcolm, Lydia Ewing, Dottis Arthur, Carolyn Dickenson, Noyal Hamilton, and Almaida Wilson, who were all indigenous Turks and Caicos Islanders.

In 1976 changes took place in Government under the new constitution and two parties were organized, namely the Progressive National Organization (PNO) and the Peoples Democratic Movement (PDM). Eligible voters went to the polls to elect Representatives for each island to form a Government that would choose a Chief Minister. With all this being completed, the Peoples Democratic Movement emerged as the ruling party and the Honourable James Alexander George Smith McCartney was appointed the First Chief Minister of the Turks and Caicos Islands. Salt Cay now had its first representative in the Government Legislative Council under the new Constitution in the person of Honourable Leon Wilson of the PDM Party.

Fig. 23 - Remains of Government House..."The Hill"

A picture showing the remains of what was once a beautiful two-storey building with many rooms. Some of the large rooms were used for parties and dances.

Police

Working along with the Government Officer was the Special Constable Mr. Wilfred Wilson, a native of Salt Cay who served for many years. I was told that there was a foreign

Very Important People and Places

Constable before him but many came after. He had his part to play in keeping law and order. Persons were brought before the Magistrate for things that one would laugh at in comparison to the now crimes. Men were charged for riding their bicycles without light or license, or for indecent language and fighting. I can recall just two serious accidents in Salt Cay that had to be tried before the Supreme Court.

After Mr. Wilson retired, Mr. James Bassett served as Special Constable for a short term. Then Police Constables, both native and foreign, were sent from the Grand Turk Police Force to serve. To name a few we had M. Taylor, S. Mohammed, F. Braithwaite, G. Worrell-Blenman, M. Lowe, T. Handfield, and Shem Clarke, who always came to talk with my Kindergarten Class. There were many more and others are constantly sent to serve in Salt Cay.

Fig. 24 - District Commissioner's Office

This is the same Office that the Government Officers occupied. During that time it was painted green and white, but has been renovated over the years and is now the District Commissioner's Office. Under this structure, there was a jail cell for use just in case anyone had to be arrested and locked away for a day or so. There is a view of the little iron bar window.

Whenever Government Dignitaries, including the Administrator, H.E. The Governor, or any other special person visited Salt Cay, it was the duty of the Government Officer to accompany them and take them around. Before there were planes and vehicles, this journey of walking about usually began when he met them on arrival at Deane's Dock and on to the school and other important places. The District Commissioners had the same tasks but some of them served at the time when the Government provided vehicles.

Our Nurses Who Served

There was a midwife who served the community in the earlier years; she either came from East Harbour or Grand Turk for a period of time to take care of her patients and deliver babies. Then two other midwives began serving the community; they were Ms. Susan Morgan and Ms. Mildred Astwood, who was the paid District Nurse. A clinic was built in the early 1950's and a nurse returned from training in Jamaica and was appointed as Midwife and Clinical Nurse. She was Nurse Nellie Glinton, who served for more than 25 years and it is believed that she delivered over 100 babies during her tenure in Salt Cay. She performed clinical duties on the island and worked with the visiting doctors. When she retired, nurses Evelyn Simmons, Camela Blenman, and many others came and went from Grand Turk and elsewhere to fill the post. In the clinic there was a dentist chair, making it possible for the dentist to make visits. When there was no clinic the dentist saw patients at Mr. Fred Morgan's house in the North District. He always visited the School to give children dental care, and adults embraced these visits for their checkups. If persons needed to see the doctor or the dentist before their scheduled visits, they had to go over to Grand Turk.

An Outstanding Head Teacher

Miss Mary C. Robinson was an outstanding personality in the island. She was among the few teachers of her time who attended Shortwood Teachers' College.

In the early 1900's there were other Head teachers, but during my school days we had a jovial, ardent, hardworking, and painstaking Head teacher who made sure that we were well taught, disciplined, and ready to move ahead. Miss Robinson served as Head teacher for over 30 years even though I was told she had come from Grand Turk in the 40's to serve a term of six months. She was there many years before I started school and was still there when I began my teaching career in 1965. She worked along with the Government Officers, helping to make most of the official events successful in Salt Cay, and she was very much involved with all the activities of the Anglican Church. Being a no-nonsense person and a disciplinarian, the entire community respected her plans and ideas, working closely with her for the welfare of the island. Although she is in her grave, her legacy speaks and lives on. In 1990 the school was renamed **MARY ROBINSON PRIMARY** in her honour. Many of us have fond memories of our school days with her. She taught some unusual things that were not in the syllabus that I don't think any other Head teacher would have thought about, and she made things happen for our school. There are many persons who attained high Government positions that were unable to attend the Secondary School, but she took us to that level *right down inside of Salt Cay*. The italicized phrase was her favourite words.

She was always ready to welcome visitors from any part of the world to our school. Whenever Ministers came to visit their churches for a weekend, she gave them an invitation to come to the school for devotions, so we looked forward to having them on Monday morning before they went back to Grand Turk. This was customary for missionaries and guest preachers, especially Bishop Eldon from the Bahamas, who always looked forward to visiting our school whenever he was in Salt Cay for the special confirmation service. When she retired in the early 70's, the school continued to move ahead with her successor, Mrs. Georgina Been. Those who followed over a period of time were Mrs. Patricia Simmons and Miss Leathe Wilson. When the population of Salt Cay began to decline as folks sought livelihood elsewhere, from then on Head teachers were sent from Grand Turk, most of them being returning residents like Anita Porter, Gwen Harvey, and Alicia Wilson.

PLACES

The Government buildings in Salt Cay included the Government Office, the primary school, and the clinic which both the dentist and doctor used during their regular visits. Most of the Church buildings are very ancient; also there are others that I would like to share about.

The White House

The White House was built in 1830 by labourers who were brought here with the salt merchants. Large Bermudian stones were brought on the boats to build this magnificent house. This attractive building, now owned by the Harriots, stands as a Historical Site and is still admired by many. You have read about this house in a previous chapter.

Churches

Although you have read concerning the churches in other chapters, I must mention the buildings as Very Important Places and other significant events and services that took place among the congregations.

The Methodist Church was a pretty big structure built in 1870 and could be seen as you walk the road going east from Deane's Dock. Many services were held in this building including the yearly Missionary Service that was very uplifting and well attended. Many special concerts were held at the church on Sunday afternoons. Various Ministers in charge of the Methodist Circuit of Churches came and went, and as a young girl I got much spiritual inspiration from Reverend Bailey, who was like a native when he visited Salt Cay. He would play the accordion and teach us many choruses even at school. Working along with the Ministers were local preachers Mr. Lloyd Been, Mr. Kenneth Garland, Mr. George Hamilton, and Mr. William Garland, who conducted many services and prayer meetings, along with the sole woman, Mrs. Japthalina Kennedy. There was the bell that rang first and second before every church service. In the yard was the Sunday School Hall that was used for many purposes including prayer meetings and revivals by overseas Evangelists. This building was renamed the **LLOYD GEORGE BEEN MEMORIAL HALL** after his death. The Church held its functions there, and it has now become the meeting place for Church Services since the main sanctuary suffered extensive damages.

Along Victoria Street in the Balfour Town you will see **ST. JOHN'S ANGLICAN CHURCH**. This building goes way back to the 1800's. Many foreign Priests came and went from this congregation also. In previous chapters, you will notice that most of the special Services on the island were held at this Church. Bishop Eldon also came from the Bahamas to conduct Confirmation Services and he always took time to visit the school. I can remember a little about the Catechist, Mr. Fred Morgan, then Mr. Wilfred Wilson, who I knew quite well. Mr. William Simmons was always keeping the doors open, ringing the bell, and keeping the lights burning. This church had quite a few lay readers and altar boys who served. Sunday School classes were held at the Hall, but many other secular functions were staged there, as well.

Fig. 25 - St. John's Anglican

Mt. Zion Baptist Church is another building that was built a long time ago. During my early years, I can remember the folks from the north moving in groups to attend special services, concerts, and prayers meetings. Many preachers and evangelists from abroad visited this congregation besides their overseas Reverends who were responsible as their ministers. Rev. Dudley Stokes of Jamaica was one who always blessed me with his sermons when we went to the church. The local leaders were Mr. Felix Dickenson, Mr. Clifford Glinton, and Rev. James Bassett, Sr., who always conducted many street meetings. This congregation had no Sunday School Hall; all of their events were held in the sanctuary and their garden parties were held in Aunt Hester Glinton's yard.

In 1967 a branch of the **Church of God of Prophecy** began to blossom in Salt Cay with Oscar Talbot as the first Pastor. He and his wife Ophelia laboured in the vineyard for many years before moving to Grand Turk. Many Revivals, District Conventions, and Street Meetings were held as Ministers, Bishops, and visiting Preachers came to conduct services and build the Ministry. They had no building of their own so they began worshipping in the little building that is now Nettie's shop, then later relocated further up the road.

Among the many important places in Salt Cay was a Guest House here in the early 1970's. This was the old **Mount Pleasant**, not the renovated, newly designed one. This house was built from 1832 but I can remember when Mr. Fred Morgan lived there during my childhood days. When Mr. James Morgan took over this house, he made it into a Guest House, the first of its kind. It was managed by Mrs. Pearl Talbot, along with her husband Earle, who worked with her, being the jack of all trades. He brought the sea foods and she prepared delicious dishes for the many guests who enjoyed being there; he was the maintenance person and security guard. Mr. Morgan had a generator in a little house in the yard and he operated that, as well.

Fig. 26 - A sketch of Mt. Pleasant Guest House when it was first opened.

Later in the early 80's Lovelace constructed and ran a little hotel at the northeastern side of the island. This was ***The Windmills***. Lastly, I must mention the place that was considered haunted. It was an old wooden house built for salt merchants, having salt stored in the cellar. That is ***The Brown House***. There was a man, Mr. Guy Black, who had a boat, the Black Douglas, anchored in front of Salt Cay in the 60's. He would come ashore and occupy this house at times. Later in the 70's Sandy Leggatt occupied this building and began repairing and renovating until it was an outstanding living quarters. This important building is now **SUNNYSIDE**.

CHAPTER 14

ALL THIS AND MORE MADE SALT CAY UNIQUE

What can I say as I try to bring closure to this book of short stories, history, and unforgettable experiences? It was a pleasure digging deep within and bringing out some of the memories that I shall never forget. It would be remiss of me not to make mention of our bush medicines – our home remedies that had great effects on the lives of people living in Salt Cay. Whenever loved ones were seriously ill or had a pain, the older folks knew that a doctor could not be reached to give advice or medicine, so they went ahead and prepared a bush medicine or two. It was then that they experimented in finding remedies for various sicknesses by using the bush medicines and nursing loved ones back to health. They would choose from the bay-tensy, Jamaica trash, catnip, dill-seed, aloes, oil tree leaves, moringa, or the yellow elder flower.

You never had far to go to find these trees; they were growing in some neighbour's yard. There were also some usual medicines that were sold in the shops, like herb tea, senna, Indian root pills, Epsom salts, Benjamin's healing oil, liniment, Vicks, Lydia Pinkham, scotch emulsion, and milk of magnesia. These medicines were either boiled or used in direct contact with the skin. In Salt Cay our parents gave us some bush medicine every Saturday, especially bay-tensy and catnip if we had consumed an excessive amount of sweets. If anyone had worms, they gave you that bush medicine for 9 consecutive mornings non-stop. Apart from that, there was a regular laxative of herb tea or senna every two or three weeks.

If we were given Indian root pills on a Friday night that was complimented with a dose of Epsom salts (donkey salts) on Saturday morning. Some days we were given a piece of aloe to swallow if we had a terrible cold, cough, or sore throat; if not that, we had to eat sugar with a few drops of Benjamin's healing oil. There were bush mixtures of all kinds during those days and they kept us all healthy with little or no expenses involved. If you have a serious sickness now, or happen to encounter one in the future, find someone from the Cay; you'll be diagnosed, given a remedy, and on your road to recovery within days.

CONCLUSION

I would have done myself and you an act of injustice to take this knowledge to heaven where it's not needed. I hope that you've enjoyed this book of humour and history, and that most of it will remain with you for a very long time. I encourage you to share what you've read with others as I have tried to give you facts as best that I could remember. I did not care to share too much beyond 1980 because by then the modern times had begun. There are many other happenings that I could have written about, but I started this book in 2003 and now that it's finally completed I'll leave the rest for another book, which perhaps someone else would find much easier to write.

May God Bless You and THANKS for believing in what I have written.

Peggy Been

SPECIAL FEATURE

AN ANTHOLOGY OF SONGS & POEMS WE ENJOYED AT SCHOOL AND IN THE COMMUNITY DURING THE YESTER YEARS

No. 1

Salt Cay a place of happy faces
With no distinction of any races
A lovely island of salt and fish
After prepared makes a delicious dish

The magnificent beaches and the crystal sea
Are things that foreigners like to see
The golden sands and the lovely shells
Are the home where the minute creatures dwell

Just take a walk down Balfour Town
And you'll see windmills as they turn around
They pump the brine from pond to pond
With the help of the sunshine salt is formed

A place of welcome and accommodation
It's rich in friendship; we love our nation
No matter how poor our island may be
It's our lovely shores that people come to see

If you're looking for a place of quiet rest
Salt Cay will be the very best

No barking of dogs, no howling of cats
Can disturb you from your quiet rest
JUST VISIT SALT CAY AND YOU WILL SEE

("The Salt Cay Calypso" written by
Thelma Kennedy & music by Leathe Wilson,
Teachers of Salt Cay Primary School in the 70's)
Used by Permission

No. 2

We dedicate this calypso
From Canada to the West Indies
By twinning School to School may we see
The world is a better place to be
Chorus:
Join hands and hearts across the seas
From Canada to the West Indies
Sing a song of Unity
And may our nations closer be

(Songs No .2 & No. 4 were songs composed at our school to share in appreciation of our twin school in Canada.)

No. 3

There is a little isle in the Turks & Caicos chain
I am sure you will join us in chanting this refrain
Whoever visit us never want to leave again
SALT CAY OUR ISLAND HOME

Special Feature

The people are so friendly they'd take you all around
To see what is going on in our little town
Where coolness and quietness and cleanliness are found
SALT CAY OUR ISLAND HOME

The beaches are inviting; you'll love them and adore
The crystal seas and the shells on the shore
If you don't have enough you can always pick some more,
SALT CAY OUR ISLAND HOME

If you live at any guesthouse you'll find a welcome there
Where maids serve you gently; there's joy beyond compare,
Sweet dishes of fish, conch, and lobster they'll prepare,
SALT CAY OUR ISLAND HOME

No matter what part of the world you chance to go
You'll enjoy your vacation in Salt Cay I know
Please come to our island; we all love you so
SALT CAY OUR ISLAND HOME
WE LOVE OUR ISLAND HOME

Words and music Ms. Leathe Wilson, Used by Permission

No. 4

Give us a land of lakes and a land of snow
And we will build Ontario
A place to live, a place to go
Ontari ari ari o
Give us a land of salt and a land of fish

Looking Back in Salt Cay

And we'll improve Salt Cay's best dish
A place to live, a place to roam
Salt Cay our little island home

<u>RING GAMES AND SONGS,
along with some ACTIONS</u>

No. 1

Steal 'em Sam; Steal 'em Sam the rocky
You steal my partner, Rocky Sam
Oh Sam, rocky Sam
You won't get none by Rocky Sam
Oh Sam rocky Sam

Actions: Everyone chooses a partner; the single person stands in the ring. As they sing he/she goes and takes someone's partner and the game continues

No. 2

A hunting we will go, a hunting we will go
We'll catch a fox and put him in a box
And never let him go

No. 3

Ask aunt Lila what she gonna cook
Peas soup and dumplings
(sing lines three times)

This song for a cultural dance…shatee

Special Feature

No. 4

Did you see Uncle Lou when he fell in the well
Oh! Oh! UNCLE Lou he fell in the well
He fell so hard that he went down to hell
Oh! Oh! Uncle Lou he fell in the well

(This song came from a true story: Uncle Lou was a young man living in Salt Cay; one day he was walking with his head in the air, flying a kite, and never realized he was close to the well until he fell in)

No. 5

Go round and round the valley,
go round and round the valley
To see your Rose again

Go in and out the window; go in and out the window
Go in and out the window, to see your Rose again

Go stand and face your lover; go stand and face your lover
Go stand and face your lover to see Rose again

Actions: As you sing one person jumps around in the ring; the same person does the actions that follow. The person chosen is the next one to go in the ring.

No. 6

All the soldiers marching through, marching through
marching through
All the soldiers marching through, sober, merrily

Take the hatchet and chop off the neck; chop off the neck; chop off the neck
Take the hatchet and chop off the neck sober, merrily

Actions: Two persons secretly choose to represent a food (e.g. ham and cheese). They make an arch with their hands; the others (soldiers) form a queue and march through as they sing. As you sing take the hatchet.... You hold one soldier who gets caught between your hands chopping around the neck. You then move her away from the others, asking "Which do you like, ham or cheese?" If its cheese, you stand behind the person who represents cheese. When everybody has been chosen, the groups do a tug of war trying to see which one is the stronger to pull over the line.

No. 7

#1	#2
Sugar you come	Yes I come again
What you bring	Piece of sugar plum
Give me piece	I ain't goin give you none
O sugar	Yes I come again,
Sweet sugar	Yes I come again

Actions: Let's call ring group #1 and person in the ring #2 replying as she has her hand on hip and waving the other. You sing this as long as you want to play this game. Keep changing ring partners.

No. 8

First time I play with trash, trash went in my eye
Second time I play with trash, trash made me cry
I went to the Governor's gate and ask him for a break
He wheel right round, and wheel right round
And give a Bahama break.... O Lolly limp O Lolly
O Lolly limp

No. 9

Polly put the kettle on kettle on kettle on
Polly put the kettle on; we'll all have tea
Here comes the red rose growing in the garden
Promised to marry me long time ago
Polly put the kettle on…we'll all have tea

Sukie take it off again off again off again
Sukie take it off again; we all gone away

POEMS & VERSES
(A select few from my school days)

No. 1

From the West Indies I have come
Salt Cay is my home
My hair is black; my eyes are bright
My skin is dark; my teeth are white.
Our Country is so very hot
Just see what nice cool clothes I've got

Salt grows in this sunny clime
Raked to export when it is time
In summer when we have no rain
The salt labourers rake the crystal grain

No. 2

I must not throw upon the floor the crust I cannot eat
For many a little hungry one may think it quite a treat
Its willful waste makes willful want, That I may live to say
Oh! How I wish I had that bread
That once I threw away

No. 3

My candle burns at both ends; it will not last the night
But oh my foes and ah my friends, it gives a lovely light

No. 4

Politeness is to do and say
The kindest thing in the kindest way

No. 5

THE GOLDEN RULE

How many ways of doing good, a little child may find
And one good way is to begin, by always being kind
Be kind to father, mother dear, for they are kind to you,
Be kind to brother, sister, friend – be kind to teacher, too

Be kind to schoolmates, kind to all, and always try to do
To each and all as you would like to have them do to you

No. 6

If I am right thy grace impart, still in the right to stay
If I am wrong, O teach my heart to find that better way

No. 7

It is easy enough to be pleasant when life flows along like a song
But the man worthwhile is the man who can smile
When everything goes dead wrong

No. 8

Have you had a kindness shown…pass it on
T'was not given for thee alone…pass it on
Let it travel down the years
Let it wipe another's tears
'Till in heaven the deed appears…pass it on

No. 9

Speak the truth and speak it ever, cause it what it will
He who hides the wrong he does, does the wrong thing still

No. 10

'Tis a lesson we must heed, try, try, try again
If at first you don't succeed, try, try, try again

No. 11

The heights of great men reached and kept
Were not attained by sudden flight
But they while their companions slept,
Were toiling upward through the night

No. 12

Lives of great men all remind us
We can make our lives sublime
And departing leave behind us
Footprints in the sands of time

No. 13

If your lips would keep from slips
Five things observe with care
To whom you speak, of whom you speak
And how and when and where

No. 14

Be kind and be gentle to those who are old
For dearer is kindness and better than gold

No. 15

Good, better, best – never let it rest
Until your good is better and your better best

Special Feature

No. 16

Labour for learning before you grow old
For knowledge is better than silver and gold
Silver and gold will vanish away
But a good education will never decay

No. 17

When wealth is lost, nothing is lost
When health is lost, something is lost
When character is lost, all is lost

No. 18

Sow a thought, reap an act
Sow an act, reap a habit
Sow a habit, reap a character
Sow a character, reap a destiny

No. 19

Do your best and be not troubled
Should some others better do
If your work should fail to please you
Don't give up but strive anew

No. 20

Let us then be up and doing
With a heart for any fate

Still achieving, still pursuing
Learn to labour and to wait

HEALTH VERSES

No. 1

Fresh air in the classroom, faces all aglow
Fresh air in the bedroom, makes us sleep – you know

No. 2

A germ dislikes the taste of soap, and water is its foe
So in your fight against disease, keep clean from head to toe

No. 3

The teeth are an index to health
All little boys and little girls, remember this I pray
To brush your teeth both noon and eve
And do it every day

No. 4

I've brushed my teeth and washed my face
And scrubbed the dirt from every nail
I've washed the soap and rinsed the bowl
And put the towel back on the rail
I've pulled my socks up smooth and straight
And rubbed my shoes to make them shine
I've brushed the dirt from coat and hat

Special Feature

And combed my hair so sleek and fine
Now that I've followed all the rules
I hope I won't be late for school

Bibliography

TURKS & Caicos Education Department, Our Country, The Turks & Caicos Islands Macmillan Caribbean 1989 (ISBN0333 47251 9)

Turks Islands Landfall, A History of the Turks & Caicos Islands by H. E Sadler--Library

Turks and Caicos Colonial Report 1953–1954
1957-1958, 1959-1960, 1967-1970, Public Library

PHOTOGRAPHS

Candy Herwin Spotlight on Salt Cay, Facebook. Used by permission.

Comedian: Story and Photo. Used by permission.

A sketch of Mount Pleasant Guest House, Salt Cay Visitors' Guide, Island Thyme, Ltd.

Turks Head Cactus and Map of Salt Cay, Turks & Caicos Annual Visitors Guide 2000, Public Library
Lighthouse Story. Used by permission.

All other photos produced personally by the author.

Acknowledgements

Dr. Beatrice Fulford
Mr. Derek "Pop" Been
Mr. G. Patrick Jarrett
Brian Riggs
Miss Leathe Wilson, Poems and Songs
Mrs. Thelma Kennedy, Poems and Songs
Mrs. Vida Talbot…Candy Recipe
Mrs. Emily "Ella" Hamilton…Bread Recipe
Jane Williams
Valerie Jennings
Winifred Jennings
Gladys Kennedy
Juanita Williams, the Librarian

Many thanks to you who assisted me in any way. To you who joggled my memory when it wasn't moving as fast as I desired. Thanks.

To God be the glory for strength, wisdom, and tenacity to follow through.

About the Author

Patronella L. Been nee Walkin comes from the beautiful little island of sun, salt and sand. She lived in Salt Cay from birth until 1987 when she migrated to Grand Turk in search of prosperity and advancement of the family.

She is known to many as "PEGGY" a childhood name given by her family and it endorses her in nearly every aspect of life throughout the Turks and Caicos Islands and beyond. She is a retired civil servant, having served as a Trained Teacher for 35 years in several Primary Schools and 5 years as Registrar of Deeds and Deputy Registrar General respectively with Turks and Caicos Government. When she retired, the experiences gained led her to Scotia Bank Turks and Caicos for another 4 years where she worked as Compliance Clerk.

Known in the community as a born again Christian and a Spiritual Leader for many years, serving God was always foremost in Patronella's life, and she continues to intercede and minister the Word in churches. In 2009 God saw it fitting to introduce her as Sister Peggy to the nation over Radio Turks and Caicos with a 5 minute daily programme 'Heart to Heart Inspirations' along with an hour of 'Sunday Inspirations'.

Reading is one of her hobbies and writing a book was always her dream; but it wasn't until 2003 that she felt passionate and excited to share about her early life in Salt Cay where she grew up with her parents, siblings and other family members. It is her greatest delight to know that her dream has become reality. To God be the glory.

Contact the Author

Please email or write the author with any comments you may have about the book.

Ms. Been is also available for book club presentations, book signings, or speaking engagements for your organization. You are welcome to contact her for bookings at:

Email:
Aboutsaltcay@gmail.com

Mailing Address:
Patronella Been
Columbus Road
Palmgrove Allotments
Grand Turk
Turks & Caicos Islands

Phone:
1 649 232 0058 or 1 649 331 5147

Notes

www.ingramcontent.com/pod-product-compliance
Lightning Source LLC
Chambersburg PA
CBHW040259170426
43193CB00020B/2949